Cambridge Elements

Elements in Decision Theory and Philosophy
edited by
Martin Peterson
Texas A&M University

THE MEASUREMENT OF SUBJECTIVE PROBABILITY

Edward J. R. Elliott
University of Leeds

CAMBRIDGE
UNIVERSITY PRESS

Shaftesbury Road, Cambridge CB2 8EA, United Kingdom

One Liberty Plaza, 20th Floor, New York, NY 10006, USA

477 Williamstown Road, Port Melbourne, VIC 3207, Australia

314–321, 3rd Floor, Plot 3, Splendor Forum, Jasola District Centre,
New Delhi – 110025, India

103 Penang Road, #05–06/07, Visioncrest Commercial, Singapore 238467

Cambridge University Press is part of Cambridge University Press & Assessment,
a department of the University of Cambridge.

We share the University's mission to contribute to society through the pursuit of
education, learning and research at the highest international levels of excellence.

www.cambridge.org
Information on this title: www.cambridge.org/9781009486965

DOI: 10.1017/9781009401319

First published 2024

A catalogue record for this publication is available from the British Library.

ISBN 978-1-009-48696-5 Hardback
ISBN 978-1-009-40132-6 Paperback
ISSN 2517-4827 (online)
ISSN 2517-4819 (print)

The Measurement of Subjective Probability

Elements in Decision Theory and Philosophy

DOI: 10.1017/9781009401319
First published online: May 2024

Edward J. R. Elliott
University of Leeds

Author for correspondence: Edward J. R. Elliott, e.j.r.elliott@leeds.ac.uk

Abstract: Beliefs come in degrees, and we often represent those degrees with numbers. We might say, for example, that we are 90 per cent confident in the truth of some scientific hypothesis, or only 30 per cent confident in the success of some risky endeavour. But what do these numbers mean? What, in other words, is the underlying psychological reality to which the numbers correspond? And what constitutes a meaningful difference between numerically distinct representations of belief? This Element discusses the main approaches to the measurement of belief. These fall into two broad categories – epistemic and decision-theoretic – with divergent foundations in the theory of measurement. Epistemic approaches explain the measurement of belief by appeal to relations between belief states themselves, whereas decision-theoretic approaches appeal to relations between beliefs and desires in the production of choice and preferences.

Keywords: measurement, subjective probability, representation theorem, qualitative probability, belief

ISBNs: 9781009486965 (HB), 9781009401326 (PB), 9781009401319 (OC)
ISSNs: 2517-4827 (online), 2517-4819 (print)

Contents

1 Introduction

It's a commonplace nowadays that beliefs come in degrees, though this isn't universally accepted. There are some holdouts – those who say the recent uptick of interest in 'credences' and 'subjective probabilities' is yet another philosophical fad that will eventually run its course. But that's hardly plausible. A very large body of work across a wide range of disciplines developed over many decades depends on the presumption that our beliefs – or something closely linked to our beliefs – admit of degrees and, moreover, that it makes good sense to represent those degrees numerically. These numerical representations of belief are far too useful for far too much to be just a passing trend.

I expect most readers will agree with me about that. But what we're much less likely to agree on is what the numbers *mean*. What is the underlying psychological reality to which these numerical representations supposedly correspond? Perspectives on this matter vary wildly. For some, degrees of belief are understood to be explicit, on-the-fly judgements about the probability of an event, or a conscious attempt to put a number on the weight of one's evidence, or the intensity of some confidence phenomenology when contemplating a possibility. Others will, like myself, think of degrees of belief as implicit attitudes – attitudes that may be present and playing a role in your cognitive economy even if you're not consciously aware of their doing so, and even if they're not readily accessible to conscious introspection. But there's a substantial variety of perspectives, too, on how these attitudes are to be understood. If I say that Ramsey believes p to degree 0.69, does that '0.69' tell us something about p's location in Ramsey's subjective confidence ordering over possibilities? Does it tell us something about Ramsey's willingness to bet on p? About the centrality of p to Ramsey's web of belief, or his dispositions to revise his opinions regarding p in the face of new evidence? All of the above? None of the above?

An intimately related (but more constrained) question concerns what's *meaningful* in a numerical representation of belief. What, in other words, does it take for numerically distinct representations to nevertheless represent the same system of beliefs? Most are happy to suppose there's no uniquely correct way to represent degrees of belief within a numerical framework, just as there's clearly no uniquely correct way to numerically represent lengths, or temperatures, or desirabilities. As Builes *et al.* (2022) recently put it,

> there's nothing '0.69-ish' about my degree of confidence in p, beyond the fact that 0.69 can serve as an adequate representation of my degree of confidence within a particular representational system. But 69, for example, or 732.6 for that matter, would work just as well, provided the system was structured in the right way. (p. 7)

But *what it is* for the representational system to be 'structured in the right way' is about as clear as mud. Here, as before, we find plentiful variation and disagreement. The most common numerical representations of belief make use of *credence functions* – mappings from propositions to real values between 0 and 1. It usually goes without saying that the relation induced over the propositions by their numerical ordering in a credence function is intended to correspond to relative strengths of belief regarding those propositions. But is that the extent of the meaningful information captured in a credence function? That is, if two credence functions are *ordinally equivalent*, does it follow that they are therefore *equivalent in meaning*? If so, then we'd probably better get started on revising the many theories of rational belief and decision making that presuppose meaningful differences between ordinally equivalent credence functions! On the other hand, if there's more to the meaning than just the numerical orderings, then exactly what additional structure *is* relevant – and why?

These are questions about the *measurement* of belief, which is the subject of this Element. In summary: what do our numerical representations of belief actually represent, how exactly do they represent it, and under what conditions are such representations meaningful?[1]

Broadly speaking, there are two main approaches to the measurement of belief. According to what I'll be calling the *epistemic approach*, a system of beliefs admits of numerical representation just in case that system has a certain kind of internal structure that can be mirrored in an appropriate numerical framework. A rather different tack – the *decision-theoretic approach* – focuses not so much on the internal structure of the belief system but instead on the relationship between beliefs, desires, and preferences in the context of decision making. Both the epistemic approach and the decision-theoretic approach can be spelled out in many different ways, but very roughly the difference between them amounts to whether the numerical representability of a system of beliefs is (a) a matter of those beliefs having a certain kind of internal coherence, or (b) a matter of those beliefs relating to preferences and desires in a coherent way. These approaches can have very different implications regarding what should and should not be considered meaningful in our numerical representations of

---

[1] The reader will note that these are not questions about the empirical process of measuring beliefs – for example, via observations of betting behaviour or survey responses. We're talking about *measurement* in the abstract sense of assigning numbers to represent quantities. The ambiguity is unfortunate, but at this point well entrenched in the literature. I'll have more to say about this in Section 3. For now, just think of the topic as relating primarily to meaningfulness in numerical representations of belief.

belief, and they can likewise diverge significantly when it comes to what an agent must be like in order for their beliefs to admit of such representations in the first place.

Cards on the table: I prefer the decision-theoretic approach. More cautiously, I would say that the decision-theoretic approach generally supplies us with the best way to interpret numerical representations of belief in the Bayesian tradition, especially in decision-theoretic contexts but also in the context of much (if not most) traditional Bayesian epistemology.[2] The basic reason for this is that standard Bayesian theories and models, and many arguments in that tradition, routinely make assumptions about meaningfulness that are hard to make sense of given the most common epistemic approaches. Further, while there *are* some less common epistemic approaches that can in principle support richer claims about meaningfulness (e.g., the multiprimitive structures discussed in Section 5.3), these are still very underdeveloped and ultimately strike me as comparatively unmotivated.

But I'll not spend a great deal of time arguing in favour of my own approach, nor arguing against the competitors. I mean – I'll do a little of that here and there, and my biases will surely be apparent in parts of the discussion, but the main purpose of this work is expositional rather than argumentative. So I'll focus much more on explaining what the epistemic and decision-theoretic approaches are, highlighting some of the possible variation within those two approaches, and the implications they have regarding what kinds of numerical representations are possible, when they're possible, and what ought to be considered meaningful in those representations.

The remainder of the discussion proceeds as follows. Section 2 introduces some key concepts from the representational theory of measurement, while Section 3 provides some clarifications and general assumptions regarding a theory of belief measurement. We then turn to the epistemic approaches: Section 4 covers the simplest version of the epistemic approach, built around binary comparative confidence relations, while Section 5 gives an overview of several alternatives. Finally, Section 6 gives an overview of the decision-theoretic approach, discusses one particular version (due to Frank Ramsey) in some detail, and addresses some common misunderstandings and objections.

---

[2] The claim here is about the majority of contexts in which numerical representations of belief actually appear, historically and today. I'm *not* asserting that the decision-theoretic approach is always or necessarily the correct approach. It would be implausible to presume that there's only one proper way to understand the numerical representation of belief for all theoretical contexts, and no doubt there will be many applications for which one or another epistemic approach would be perfectly apt (cf. Section 2.4, on conventionality in measurement).

2 Representation and Measurement

We find it abundantly useful to express many physical facts using numbers and numerical relations. There's no great mystery to this, even for the mathematical Platonist who thinks that numbers and numerical relations are abstracta and not present in the physical world in the same manner as electrons or chairs or gravitational attraction. When I say I've gained *at least 2 pounds* thanks to all the nice food at a recent conference, which is *more than twice as much* as what I gained at the last conference, I'm using those numbers and numerical relations to refer to and reason about my ever-increasing weight. These claims aren't made true by virtue of any little numbers attached somewhere to my body, slowly and inevitably going up over time. Rather, the numbers and numerical relations serve as abstract stand-ins for physical properties and physical relations, and they do this by virtue of some structural similarity between them.

What we call *quantities* are determinable properties whose determinates have a certain salient relational structure that renders them ripe for numerical representation. Length, for instance, is a determinable attribute, with determinates – the specific lengths – sharing higher-order relations between them that can be usefully represented within a numerical framework. For any two physical objects o and o' and a fixed orientation for each, either (a) o will be at least as long as o', or (b) o' will be at least as long as o, or (c) both (i.e., they'll be as long as each other). Here, the *at least as long* relation holds between physical objects, but we can also understand it as a second-order relation between the length attributes directly. Say that any two objects have the same length, L, if each is at least as long as the other. Say next that L is *at least as long* as L' just in case any object with property L is at least as long as any object with property L'. We can then associate the lengths L and L' with numbers x and y in such a manner that L is at least as long as L' just in case $x \geq y$.

In this example, the lengths L, L' and the *at least as long* relation between them are said to be *qualitative*, whereas the numbers x, y and the $\geq$ relation between them serve as their *numerical* representations. Think of a qualitative property or relation as one that can be characterised without explicit reference to numbers or numerical relations. So 'qualitative' here contrasts with 'numerical', not with 'quantitative' – the idea being that quantities can be characterised either in qualitative terms or in numerical terms, with the latter being possible precisely because the abstract numerical stuff shares a structure in common with the real-world qualitative stuff it represents.[3]

---

[3]　This usage of 'qualitative' is common in the literature. Some will say that a numerical system is defined by its structure, and hence anything with the same structure instantiates that system

The purpose of this section is to expand on that initial idea and make it more precise. More generally, the goal is to introduce some key concepts for discussing the numerical representation of quantities. I start with the fundamentals of the Representational Theory of Measurement (RTM).[4]

2.1 Preliminary Concepts

I presume familiarity with predicate logic, and with the elementary concepts and notation of set theory. Much of what follows will revolve around properties of binary relations and operations, though, so the following are worth stating:

Definition 1. An *n*-ary relation on a set $\mathbf{X}$ is a subset of $\mathbf{X}^n$. Where $R \subseteq \mathbf{X} \times \mathbf{X}$, by convention, xRy if and only if $(x, y) \in R$ and $x\cancel{R}y$ if and only if $(x, y) \notin R$. We say that R is

- *transitive* if and only if xRy and yRz implies xRz, for all $x, y, z \in \mathbf{X}$,
- *complete* if and only if xRy or yRx for all $x, y \in \mathbf{X}$,
- *reflexive* if and only if xRx, for all $x \in \mathbf{X}$,
- *symmetric* if and only if xRy implies yRx, for all $x, y \in \mathbf{X}$,
- *asymmetric* if and only if xRy implies not yRx, for all $x, y \in \mathbf{X}$,
- *antisymmetric* if and only if xRy and yRx implies $x = y$, for all $x, y \in \mathbf{X}$,
- a *preorder* if and only if R is transitive and reflexive,
- a *weak order* if and only if R is a complete preorder,
- a *total order* if and only if R is an antisymmetric weak order, and
- an *equivalence relation* if and only if R is transitive, reflexive, and symmetric.

Furthermore, where $\succsim$ is defined on a set $\mathbf{X}$, then x is said to be

- *minimal* (in $\succsim$) if and only if $y \succsim x$ for all $y \in \mathbf{X}$, and
- *maximal* (in $\succsim$) if and only if $x \succsim y$ for all $y \in \mathbf{X}$.

Preorders – especially weak orders – will be important. Throughout, I'll use $\succsim$ to represent a number of qualitative preorder relations, and I'll use $\sim$ and $>$ for the symmetric and asymmetric parts of $\succsim$ respectively. That is, I'll henceforth take it as read that

---

and should also be considered 'numerical' (e.g., Michell 2021). That may be right. But what I have to say won't hinge on whether 'qualitative' systems *instantiate* 'numerical' systems or are *represented by* them, and either way the terminological distinction is useful.

[4] The locus classicus for the RTM is Krantz *et al.* (1971); see also Suppes and Zinnes (1963), Pfanzagl (1968), Narens (1985), and Roberts (1985).

- $x \sim y$ if and only if $x \gtrsim y$ and $y \gtrsim x$, and
- $x > y$ if and only if $x \gtrsim y$ and $y \not\gtrsim x$.

Definition 2. An n-ary operation on a set $\mathbf{X}$ is a (total or partial) function from $\mathbf{X}^n$ into $\mathbf{X}$. Suppose $\bullet$ is a binary operation on $\mathbf{X}$. By convention, $x \bullet y = z$ if and only if $\bullet(x,y) = z$, and $x \bullet y$ is *defined* if and only if $\bullet(x,y)$ is defined. Furthermore, we say that $\bullet$ is

- *total* if and only if $x \bullet y$ is defined for all $x, y \in \mathbf{X}$, otherwise *partial*,
- *commutative* if and only if $\bullet$ is total and for all $x, y \in \mathbf{X}$, $x \bullet y = y \bullet x$, and
- *associative* if and only if $\bullet$ is total and for all $x, y \in \mathbf{X}$, $x \bullet (y \bullet z) = (x \bullet y) \bullet z$.

Note that *properties* are just the special case of n-ary relations where $n = 1$, and every n-ary operation can be recast as an $(n+1)$-ary relation. For example, addition is a total binary operation on the set of real numbers $\mathbb{R}$, since it maps $\mathbb{R} \times \mathbb{R}$ back into $\mathbb{R}$; it is also the ternary relation R on $\mathbb{R}$ such that $(x, y, z) \in R$ if and only if $x + y = z$. As such, for what follows I'll usually just write 'relations' rather than 'properties and relations' or 'relations and operations' – but wherever I intend to refer to operations in particular, this will be explicitly marked.

Next we need the generic notion of a *relational system*. This is a system comprising a set, one or more distinguished relations on that set, and zero or more distinguished binary operations:

Definition 3. Let $\mathbf{I}$ ($\supset \varnothing$) and $\mathbf{J}$ ($\supseteq \varnothing$) be index sets. Then $\langle \mathbf{X}, R_i; \bullet_j \rangle_{j \in \mathbf{J}}^{i \in \mathbf{I}}$ is a *relational system* if and only if $\mathbf{X}$ is a non-empty set, the R_i are relations on $\mathbf{X}$, and the $\bullet_j$ are binary operations on $\mathbf{X}$.

The relations and operations used to characterise a relational system are known as the *primitives* of that system. Note the semi-colon, used to explicitly separate the primitive relations from the primitive operations.[5]

An example of a simple relational system is $\langle \mathbb{R}, \geq \rangle$, comprising the set $\mathbb{R}$ and the primitive *at least as great* relation $\geq$ on $\mathbb{R}$. A richer relational system would be $\langle \mathbb{R}, \geq; + \rangle$, which includes also the primitive binary operation $+$. These are what we'll call *numerical systems* – they're comprised of a set of numbers and one or more relations thereupon. More generally, we take a numerical system

---

[5] I've followed Roberts (1985) rather than Krantz *et al.* (1971) for how I define relational systems. Doing so allows for a distinction between weak and strong homomorphisms (Definition 4), which helps avoid some minor issues arising in connection to the representation of partial operations and non-antisymmetric preorders.

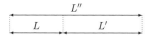

Figure 1 L'' is the end-to-end concatenation of L and L' (i.e., $L \circ L' = L''$).

to be any relational system constructed from numerical stuff. (There's no need to be very precise here – some relational systems have a numerical feel about them, and that'll suffice for referring to them as numerical systems.) In contrast are *qualitative systems*, or systems constructed from qualitative stuff. For example, if **L** is the set of determinate length properties (as described at the beginning of the section), and $\succsim$ is the *at least as long* relation between them, then $\langle \mathbf{L}, \succsim \rangle$ will count as a qualitative system. Likewise, for any two lengths L and L', we let their *end-to-end concatenation*, $L \circ L'$, be the length L'' of any object that's as long as what you get when you take two disjoint rigid objects of length L and L' and attach them end-to-end. (See Figure 1.) Then $\circ$ will be a binary operation on **L**, and $\langle \mathbf{L}, \succsim; \circ \rangle$ will also be a qualitative system.

Henceforth, I'll use $\mathcal{N}$ for numerical systems and $\mathcal{Q}$ for qualitative systems. We need then a way of expressing when a qualitative relational system possesses a similar structure to that of some numerical system, such that the latter might be exploited to represent the former. For this we make use of *structure-preserving mappings*, or *homomorphisms*:

Definition 4. Let $\mathcal{Q} = \langle \mathbf{X}, R_i; \bullet_j \rangle$ and $\mathcal{N} = \langle \mathbf{Y}, S_i; *_j \rangle$, where $i \in \mathbf{I}$ and $j \in \mathbf{J}$. Then $\varphi \colon \mathbf{X} \mapsto \mathbf{Y}$ is a *weak homomorphism from $\mathcal{Q}$ into $\mathcal{N}$* if and only if

1. R_i is an n-ary relation if and only if S_i is an n-ary relation
2. $(x_1, \ldots, x_n) \in R_i$ if and only if $(\varphi(x_1), \ldots, \varphi(x_n)) \in S_i$
3. $\varphi(x \bullet_j y) = \varphi(x) *_j \varphi(y)$

φ is a *strong homomorphism from $\mathcal{Q}$ into $\mathcal{N}$* if, in addition,

4. $x \bullet_j y = z$ if and only if $\varphi(x) *_j \varphi(y) = \varphi(z)$

Corresponding to the distinction between weak homomorphisms and strong homomorphisms, we can say that φ *weakly maps* $\bullet$ into $*$ whenever

$$x \bullet y = z \text{ implies } \varphi(x) * \varphi(y) = \varphi(z).$$

and *strongly maps* $\bullet$ into $*$ whenever the converse also holds.

An example will help to make this clearer. Start first with the simple qualitative system $\langle \mathbf{L}, \succsim \rangle$. A function $\varphi \colon \mathbf{L} \mapsto \mathbb{R}$ is a homomorphism from $\langle \mathbf{L}, \succsim \rangle$ into $\langle \mathbb{R}, \geq \rangle$ when

$$L \succsim L' \text{ if and only if } \varphi(L) \geq \varphi(L').$$

Since there are no primitive operations in $\langle \mathbf{L}, \succsim \rangle$, conditions 3 and 4 are trivially satisfied and so we don't bother with the weak/strong distinction. Next, consider the richer system $\langle \mathbf{L}, \succsim; \circ \rangle$, this time endowed with a primitive concatenation operation. This time, then, a function $\varphi \colon \mathbf{L} \mapsto \mathbb{R}$ counts as a weak homomorphism from $\langle \mathbf{L}, \succsim; \circ \rangle$ into $\langle \mathbb{R}, \geq; + \rangle$ whenever, in addition to the preceding, it weakly maps $\circ$ into $+$:

$$\varphi(L \circ L') = \varphi(L) + \varphi(L').$$

And φ is a strong homomorphism if it strongly maps $\circ$ into $+$:

$$\varphi(L) + \varphi(L') = \varphi(L'') \text{ if and only if } L \circ L = L''$$

If $\circ$ is a total operation and $\succsim$ is antisymmetric, then every weak homomorphism from $\langle \mathbf{L}, \succsim; \circ \rangle$ into $\langle \mathbb{R}, \geq; + \rangle$ will be a strong homomorphism – but otherwise this needn't be the case.

2.2 Representation Theorems and Uniqueness

A homomorphism maps the primitive relations and operations of one relational system into the primitive relations and operations of another. When at least a weak homomorphism from Q into N exists, we can say that N has – or otherwise includes as a proper part – a structure similar to that of Q. A strong homomorphism establishes a slightly stronger similarity of structure. In either case, it is this similarity that justifies representing Q using (or 'in') N. Because of this, the central theoretical objects of the RTM are results that establish precise conditions for when an arbitrary qualitative system Q can be represented in some specific numerical system N. These are known as *representation theorems*.

Let $\Phi(Q, N)$ denote the set of all weak homomorphisms from Q into N. Then, for a prespecified N, a representation theorem supplies (at least) sufficient conditions on Q to guarantee that some such homomorphism exists. The conditions are usually called the *axioms* of that theorem. Typically, the axioms will be chosen such that (at least) most of them are individually necessary for representability – that is, they're direct consequences of the assumption that $\Phi(Q, N)$ is non-empty. Axioms that are not necessary for representability are usually known as *structural* axioms.[6] For example:

---

[6] Be careful: an axiom may be necessary *for a representation theorem*, but not necessary *for representability*. This is because representation theorems often do more than simply assert sufficient conditions for representability.

Theorem 5 (Krantz et al. 1971, 15) *Let* **X** *be a set and* $\succsim$ *a binary relation on* **X**. *Then there is at least one homomorphism from* $\langle \mathbf{X}, \succsim \rangle$ *into* $\langle \mathbb{R}, \geq \rangle$ *if*

1. **X** *is finite* (finitude)
2. $\succsim$ *is a weak order* (weak order)

The *weak order* axiom is necessary: since $\geq$ is a weak order on $\mathbb{R}$, if **X** is to be mapped into $\mathbb{R}$ then $\succsim$ must itself be a weak order if it's to be mapped into $\geq$. The *finitude* axiom is structural – it's possible to represent $\langle \mathbf{X}, \succsim \rangle$ in $\langle \mathbb{R}, \geq \rangle$ even if **X** is infinite, though in that case additional axioms are needed to ensure representability. (See Krantz *et al.* (1971), 40–1, for details.)

A representation theorem will also usually include or otherwise be associated with a *uniqueness result*. In the ideal case, the uniqueness result tells us about the relationship between homomorphisms belonging to $\mathbf{\Phi}(Q, \mathcal{N})$ for all Q satisfying the axioms of the associated representation theorem. Continuing the example, it's plain to see that if φ is any homomorphism from $\langle \mathbf{X}, \succsim \rangle$ into $\langle \mathbb{R}, \geq \rangle$, then so too is $\psi : \mathbf{X} \mapsto \mathbb{R}$ if and only if

$\psi(x) \geq \psi(y)$ if and only if $\varphi(x) \geq \varphi(y)$.

Any ψ satisfying this condition is related to φ by a *strictly increasing* (or order-preserving) transformation. So the kind of uniqueness result we'd expect to find attached to Theorem 5 would say that *given weak order and finitude*, the homomorphisms in $\mathbf{\Phi}(\langle \mathbf{X}, \succsim \rangle, \langle \mathbb{R}, \geq \rangle)$ are *unique up to an order-preserving transformation*. The 'unique up to' phrasing is another way to say that the homomorphism set is constrained by the specified transformation – hence it designates a property shared by all and only the functions in the set.

Two points of caution. First: a uniqueness result applies to all systems *satisfying the axioms of the associated representation theorem* – not necessarily to all systems that are representable in the specified numerical system *simpliciter*. This is important if the representation theorem includes structural axioms, which are sometimes used to strengthen the uniqueness result. As a rule of thumb, the more structural constraints imposed on Q, the more restricted the potential homomorphisms from Q into $\mathcal{N}$, leading to a stronger uniqueness result. Second: many uniqueness results apply only to a proper subset of the possible homomorphisms in $\mathbf{\Phi}(Q, \mathcal{N})$. For example, the uniqueness result may assert that there is only one homomorphism from $\langle \mathbf{X}, \succsim \rangle$ into $\langle \mathbb{R}, \geq \rangle$ *which satisfies such-and-such properties* (e.g., *is a probability measure*), even while there are infinitely many homomorphisms in $\mathbf{\Phi}(Q, \mathcal{N})$ that do not. For these reasons, one must be careful when interpreting a uniqueness result – some results that on first glance appear rather impressive may end up only really reflecting the

Table 1 Scale types and uniqueness conditions

Scale type	Uniqueness condition	Relations preserved
Ordinal	Strictly increasing transformations	Orderings
Interval	Positive affine transformations	Difference ratios
Ratio	Positive similarity transformations	Ratios
Absolute	Identity	Everything

strength of the structural conditions employed in the representation theorem and/or arbitrary restrictions to a particular representational format.

Moving on – the final thing to do in this section is outline the major *scale types*. (See Table 1.) In the preceding example, the φ in $\mathbf{\Phi}(Q, \mathcal{N})$ are unique up to order-preserving transformations. In that case, the set $\mathbf{\Phi}(Q, \mathcal{N})$ is said to be an *ordinal scale* of Q, and the φ in $\mathbf{\Phi}(Q, \mathcal{N})$ are also called *ordinal scales* of Q. (The ambiguity is unfortunate, but context usually suffices for disambiguation.) Three other scale types are also important. The next is an *interval scale*: $\mathbf{\Phi}(Q, \mathcal{N})$ is an *interval scale* when the $\varphi \in \mathbf{\Phi}(Q, \mathcal{N})$ are unique up to a *positive affine* (or interval-preserving) transformation – that is, if $\varphi \in \mathbf{\Phi}(Q, \mathcal{N})$ then so is ψ, for any ψ defined such that for some real values r and s, with $r > 0$,

$$\psi(x) = r\varphi(x) + s.$$

Whereas order-preserving transformations merely preserve orderings, interval-preserving transformations preserve ratios of differences (and thus also orderings). So, if φ and ψ are related by an interval-preserving transformation, then

$$\frac{\varphi(x) - \varphi(y)}{\varphi(z) - \varphi(w)} = \frac{\psi(x) - \psi(y)}{\psi(z) - \psi(w)}.$$

Next are *ratio scales*: $\mathbf{\Phi}(Q, \mathcal{N})$ is a ratio scale when the $\varphi \in \mathbf{\Phi}(Q, \mathcal{N})$ are unique up to a *positive similarity* (or ratio-preserving) transformation – that is, if φ is in $\mathbf{\Phi}(Q, \mathcal{N})$, then so is ψ, for any ψ defined such that for some real value $r > 0$,

$$\psi(x) = r\varphi(x).$$

Ratio-preserving transformations preserve ratios (and thus also ratios of differences, and thus also orderings). So, if φ and ψ are related by a ratio-preserving transformation, then

$$\frac{\varphi(x)}{\varphi(y)} = \frac{\psi(x)}{\psi(y)}.$$

Finally, there are *absolute scales*. This is just the case where $\mathbf{\Phi}(Q, \mathcal{N})$ contains exactly one homomorphism.

The foregoing classification scheme originates with Stevens (1946). It's the most widely known means of classifying scale types by a wide margin. It works well for most purposes, and it'll suffice for ours, though it's not the only classification scheme nor is it the most general. (A more general classification scheme, though also more complicated, can be found in Narens (1981).)

2.3 Extensive and Conjoint Measurement

Of special interest to the theory of measurement are 'additive' representations. Roughly, these are representations that make use of addition in some important way. It can be a little hard to define precisely, though, as what it takes for a representation to count as 'additive' can vary across measurement structures. The simplest case is that of *extensive measurement*. Here, we can say that a homomorphism from Q into N is *weakly additive* when it weakly maps one of Q's primitives into addition; *strong additivity* can then be defined in the obvious parallel way. The qualitative operation that gets mapped into addition is usually referred to as a *concatenation* operation.

Let's discuss one example of an extensive measurement structure in more detail – a *positive concatenation structure*. Since it doesn't make sense to speak of lengths shorter than no length at all, we conventionally measure length using additive homomorphisms from $\langle \mathbf{L}, \gtrsim; \circ \rangle$ into $\langle \mathbb{R}^{\geq 0}, \geq; + \rangle$, where $\mathbb{R}^{\geq 0}$ is the set of real numbers not smaller than zero. The *metre scale* is one such homomorphism. Let L_m be the *metre length*, defined as the length of the path light travels in a vacuum in $1/299,792,458$ of a second. Then the metre scale, φ_m, corresponds to the (unique) strong homomorphism from $\langle \mathbf{L}, \gtrsim; \circ \rangle$ into $\langle \mathbb{R}^{\geq 0}, \geq; + \rangle$ that assigns the unit value to L_m. In other words,

1. $\varphi_m(L) \geq 0$ and $\varphi_m(L_m) = 1$
2. $L \geq L'$ if and only if $\varphi_m(L) \geq \varphi_m(L')$
3. $L \circ L' = L''$ if and only if $\varphi_m(L) + \varphi_m(L') = \varphi_m(L'')$

This method of measuring length is possible precisely because the behaviour of $\gtrsim$ and $\circ$ is mirrored by the behaviour of $+$ and $\geq$ over the non-negative reals. The most important conditions are as follows:

1. $\gtrsim$ is a weak order   (*weak order*)
2. $L \circ (L' \circ L'') = (L \circ L') \circ L''$ (*associativity*)
3. $L \circ L' = L' \circ L$ (*commutativity*)
4. $L \gtrsim L'$ if and only if $L \circ L'' \gtrsim L' \circ L''$ (*monotonicity*)
5. $L \circ L' \gtrsim L$ (*weak positivity*)
6. $L \circ L' \sim L$ only if L' is minimal in $\gtrsim$ (*identity element*)

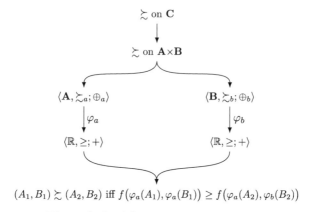

Figure 2 Conjoint measurement structure

Compare, for $x, y, z \in \mathbb{R}^{\geq 0}$:

1. $\geq$ is a weak order   (*weak order*)
2. $x + (y + z) = (x + y) + z$ (*associativity*)
3. $x + y = y + x$ (*commutativity*)
4. $x \geq y$ if and only if $x + z \geq y + z$ (*monotonicity*)
5. $x + y \geq x$ (*weak positivity*)
6. $x + y = x$ only if $y = 0$ (*identity element*)

Epistemic approaches to the measurement of belief focus on representing the internal structure of the belief system, and typically posit systems that look a great deal like positive concatenation structures. However, not all 'additive' representations follow the same model – they do not all require a primitive concatenation operation that gets mapped into addition. An alternative way to generate 'additive' representations employs *conjoint measurement structures*, wherein multiple quantities are represented simultaneously and the additive structure of the representation is derived from the nature of their lawlike relationships. Since conjoint measurement is important for decision-theoretic approaches to the measurement of belief, it's worth considering an example in a bit of detail. The procedure is more complicated than the case of extensive measurement (see Figure 2).[7]

---

[7] The example is chosen to highlight a few key ideas; it's far from the only conjoint measurement structure and it's different in certain respects from some decision-theoretic structures. As with extensive measurement, there's a wide variety of conjoint measurement structures and a correspondingly wide variety of numerical systems within which they might be represented.

We start with a single weak ordering, $\gtrsim$, defined for some quantity **C** that's determined by two independent factors **A** and **B**. For example, suppose **C** is discomfort as determined by temperature **A** and humidity **B** (Krantz *et al.* 1971, 17–18), momentum as determined by mass and velocity (Luce & Tukey 1964, 4–5), or overall value as determined by monetary and sentimental value.

In any case, we suppose $\gtrsim$ on **C** is determined by these two factors **A** and **B**, whatever they may all be. Formally we can represent this by reconstructing $\gtrsim$ as an ordering not over **C** directly but instead over **A**×**B**. So, for example,

$$(A_1, B_1) \gtrsim (A_2, B_2)$$

is understood to mean that the level of **C** determined by the combination of A_1 and B_1 is at least as great as the level of **C** determined by A_2 and B_2, where the A_1, A_2 and B_1, B_2 are levels of **A** and **B** respectively.

The next step is to extract from $\gtrsim$ two extensive 'subsystems' for **A** and **B** separately. We start by defining an ordering $\gtrsim_a$ over **A**, by comparing the levels of **C** that result from varying the **A** factor while holding the **B** factor fixed. That is,

$$A_1 \gtrsim_a A_2 \text{ iff } (A_1, B_i) \gtrsim (A_2, B_i) \text{ for all } B_i \in \mathbf{B}.$$

So A_1 is greater than A_2 when A_1 contributes more to **C** than A_2 does, holding the level of **B** fixed. Note, of course, that the definition alone doesn't guarantee $\gtrsim_a$ will be a weak order – for that we need to suppose that if changing from A_1 to A_2 increases the level of **C** while holding the level of **B** fixed for any particular level of **B**, then the same should hold for all levels of **B**. Essentially this amounts to saying that the contribution **A** makes to **C** is independent of the contribution made by **B**. This is established by the *independence* axiom, which will be explained in a later paragraph. An exactly parallel definition gets us an ordering $\gtrsim_b$ over **B**.

At this point we've got two very simple subsystems, $\langle \mathbf{A}, \gtrsim_a \rangle$ and $\langle \mathbf{B}, \gtrsim_b \rangle$. But we should like to construct extensive structures so as to enable a richer numerical representation. Thus we will need to define a concatenation operation as well. Assume that **A** and **B** combine in an intuitively 'additive' fashion. (This will be qualitatively expressed by means of the *independence* and *double cancellation* axioms.) Then, it will be possible to draw meaningful correlations in size between intervals in $\gtrsim_a$ and in $\gtrsim_b$ by comparing the effects on the level of **C** that result from varying one factor while holding the other fixed. For suppose there are A_1, A_2, B_1, B_2 such that

$$(A_1, B_2) \sim (A_2, B_1) > (A_1, B_1).$$

We can read this as saying that changing from A_1 to A_2 (while holding the **B**-level fixed) has the same effect on **C** as changing from B_1 to B_2 (while holding the **A**-level fixed). If we let $A_i \rightarrow A_j$ designate the interval between A_i and A_j as observed in the effect on **C**, and likewise for $B_i \rightarrow B_j$ mutatis mutandis, then what we've said is that $A_1 \rightarrow A_2$ is equal to $B_1 \rightarrow B_2$, and thus we compare the size of intervals in one factor to intervals in the other. Given that, if there also are minimal levels A_0 and B_0 of **A** and **B**, then we can define concatenation operations $\oplus_a$ and $\oplus_b$ for each of **A** and **B**. Starting with $\oplus_a$, we say

$$A_1 \oplus_a A_2 = A_3$$

just in case the effect on **C** that results from increasing A_0 to A_3 while holding the level of **B** fixed at B_0 is equal to the effect on **C** that results from increasing the level of **A** from A_0 to A_1 and increasing the level of **B** from B_0 to some level B_x such that the result is equal in effect on **C** as observed from an increase from A_0 to A_2. That is, if

$$(A_3, B_0) \sim (A_1, B_x),$$

then $A_0 \rightarrow A_3$ is equal to $A_0 \rightarrow A_1$ plus $B_0 \rightarrow B_x$, where the latter is known to be equal to $A_0 \rightarrow A_2$. Treating A_0 and B_0 as 'zero' points, then, the 'size' of the interval $A_0 \rightarrow A_i$ gives the absolute 'size' of A_i alone, and so this essentially amounts to saying that A_3 equals A_1 plus A_2.

The upshot is that, with the appropriate axioms on $\succsim$, we can extract extensive subsystems $\langle \mathbf{A}, \succsim_a; \oplus_a \rangle$ and $\langle \mathbf{B}, \succsim_b; \oplus_a \rangle$ out of the initial system $\langle \mathbf{A} \times \mathbf{B}, \succsim \rangle$, which will admit of separate additive representations φ_a and φ_b. The final step is to then show that there exists some numerical operation, f, that combines φ_a and φ_b so as to represent $\succsim$ on $\mathbf{A} \times \mathbf{B}$; that is,

$$(A_1, B_1) \succsim (A_2, B_2) \text{ if and only if } f\big(\varphi_a(A_1), \varphi_b(B_1)\big) \geq f\big(\varphi_a(A_2), \varphi_b(B_2)\big).$$

The function f may take a wide variety of forms depending on the shape of $\succsim$, but one simple case is when φ_a and φ_b combine additively to determine a final value that represents **C**:

$$(A_1, B_1) \succsim (A_2, B_2) \text{ if and only if } \varphi_a(A_1) + \varphi_a(B_1) \geq \varphi_a(A_2) + \varphi_b(B_2)$$

The result is a *conjoint* representation of all three quantities **A**, **B**, and **C** simultaneously, achieved via a two-component vector homomorphism φ from $\langle \mathbf{A} \times \mathbf{B}, \succsim \rangle$ into $\langle \mathbb{R} \times \mathbb{R}, \geq \rangle$ that 'decomposes' into φ_a and φ_b via f.

All of this obviously requires that $\succsim$ will satisfy the axioms required for the existence of such a representation. These axioms will together essentially assert that $\succsim$ behaves in the manner one would expect if levels of **C** were determined by the sum of two independent factors **A** and **B**. For instance, the following are very typical necessary axioms for additive conjoint measurement structures:

1. For all $A_i, A_j, A_k, A_l \in$ **A** and $B_i, B_j, B_k, B_l \in$ **B**, $(A_i, B_k) \gtrsim (A_j, B_k)$ if and only if $(A_i, B_l) \gtrsim (A_j, B_l)$, and $(A_k, B_i) \gtrsim (A_k, B_j)$ if and only if $(A_l, B_i) \gtrsim (A_l, B_j)$
   (*independence*)
2. For all $A_i, A_j, A_k \in$ **A** and $B_i, B_j, B_k \in$ **B**, $(A_i, B_j) \gtrsim (A_j, B_k)$ and $(A_j, B_i) \gtrsim (A_k, B_j)$ implies $(A_i, B_i) \gtrsim (A_k, B_k)$
   (*double cancellation*)

Again, it's helpful to compare the qualitative axiom with the intended numerical representation. The *independence* axiom is straightforward:

$$x + z \geq y + z \text{ for some } z$$
$$\downarrow$$
$$x + z \geq y + z \text{ for all } z$$

The *double cancellation* axiom is a little less obvious; it concerns cases in which the common terms of two inequalities cancel out to determine a third:

$$x + m \geq y + o$$
$$y + n \geq z + m$$
$$\downarrow$$
$$x + n \geq z + o$$

Let's sum up. In the example of a conjoint measurement structure I've just outlined, the numerical representations of **A**, **B**, and **C** are a package deal. Or, more accurately, they're three parts of a single representational system comprising several functions and an operation that ties them together. Note in particular – and this will be important – that the two constructed subsystems are defined such that they only make sense as parts of the larger system. The primitives of $\langle$**A**, $\gtrsim_a; \oplus_a\rangle$, for instance, are characterised in terms of how **A** relates to **B** in the determination of **C**. Likewise, the operation $\oplus_a$ needn't correspond to any 'natural' concatenation operation that can be readily defined in terms of **A** alone, without reference to how **A** interacts with **B** and **C**. To the extent that **A** is represented as having an 'additive' structure in this manner, then, that structure is manifest in its relationship with **B** and **C**. This is all to say that the *meaning* of the representation φ_a in this context can only be fully grasped by reference to its relation to φ_b as specified by the rule f by which they combine to represent **C**. The three numerical representations are, in that sense, inseparable.

Contrast this with the extensive measurement of $\langle$**L**, $\gtrsim; \circ\rangle$, where the primitives of that system can be characterised without any direct reference to other quantities. One can appreciate what it is for the system of lengths to have an 'additive' structure just by considering how determinate length attributes relate to other determinate length attributes. One needn't embed the system of lengths into a larger relational structure involving multiple quantities in order to comprehend what it is for one length to be *twice as long* as another, for example, since one can just *see it* directly by placing the lengths alongside one another. An intuitive way to characterise the difference between the two kinds of measurement structure, then, is to say extensive measurement is geared towards representing the internal relational structure of a single determinable attribute, whereas the conjoint measurement is geared more towards representing the relationships between several attributes.

2.4 Conventionality

One of the more important lessons of the RTM concerns the extent to which our use of numbers to represent the world is grounded in convention. (By 'conventional', I mean *unforced from a purely mathematical point of view*, and so setting aside pragmatic considerations.) It's useful to divide it up into three distinct *grades of conventionality*.

Most will be plenty familiar already with conventionality of the first grade, *choice of scale* – that is, in the choice of homomorphism from $\Phi(Q, \mathcal{N})$, for a fixed choice of Q and $\mathcal{N}$. This arises, for instance, when we are free to choose between *metres*, *inches*, *light-years*, or *beard-seconds* (the amount a typical beard grows in one second) as our units for measuring length.

A rather deeper and not as widely appreciated form of conventionality arises in the *choice of numerical system*. A very simple example is the choice to use $\geq$ to represent a weak order $\succsim$, rather than $\leq$. Either would obviously work just as well as the other – and just as well as any other weak order on the reals. But a more complicated example is also worth mentioning. As I noted in the previous section, conventional measures of length are almost always additive homomorphisms from $\langle \mathbf{L}, \succsim; \circ \rangle$ to $\langle \mathbb{R}, \geq; + \rangle$. On any such measure, the value assigned to $L \circ L$ will always be *twice* the value assigned to L. Our overwhelming familiarity with these additive measures can lead to the sense that there's something uniquely correct about this representation – that the qualitative relation holding between L and $L \circ L$ is an essentially *twice*-ish relation. As Brian Ellis (1968, 83) put it, there's a common sense that the 'twice' in 'twice as long' has a significance independent of the conventions of measurement. ('Clearly, 2 meters is *twice as long* as long as 1 meter – that is the natural and obvious way to describe their relation!') However, the axioms that justify the additive measurement of length – *associativity*, *commutativity*, *monotonicity*, and so on – are consistent with a multitude of non-additive representations whereby $L \circ L$ need not be assigned a value twice that which is assigned to L.

Consider multiplicative measures, which map $\langle \mathbf{L}, \gtrsim; \circ \rangle$ not into $\langle \mathbb{R}^{\geq 0}, \geq; + \rangle$ but into $\langle \mathbb{R}^{\geq 1}, \geq; \times \rangle$ instead (see Hölder 1901; Krantz *et al.* 1971, 11–12, 99ff; Narens 1985, 27–31). Let the multiplicative (base 2) version of the metre scale be called the *schmetre scale*; it corresponds to a homomorphism φ_{sch} that maps $\langle \mathbf{L}, \gtrsim; \circ \rangle$ onto $\langle \mathbb{R}^{\geq 1}, \geq; \times \rangle$ such that

1. $\varphi_{sch}(L) \geq 1$ and $\varphi_{sch}(L_m) = 2$
2. $L \geq L'$ if and only if $\varphi_{sch}(L) \geq \varphi_{sch}(L')$
3. $L \circ L' = L''$ if and only if $\varphi_{sch}(L) \times \varphi_{sch}(L') = \varphi_{sch}(L'')$

On the schmetre scale, the value assigned to $L \circ L$ will always be equal to the square of the value assigned to L. Since 1 metre is 2 schmetres, then, 2 metres is 4 schmetres and 4 metres is 16 schmetres. Hence, if 4 metres is *twice as long* as 2 metres, it follows that 16 schmetres is *twice as long* as 4 schmetres. The point is not that there's some sort of contradiction here – there isn't. Rather, it's that the qualitative relation between $L \circ L$ and L is no more a *twice*-ish relation than it is a *square*-ish relation. Our use of 'twice as long' to refer to and describe the relation between $L \circ L$ and L reflects only a conventional preference for additive representations over an infinite variety of alternative representational formats that are, from a mathematical point of view, equally adequate to the task.

But the conventionality runs deeper still, for it arises also in the *choice of qualitative system*. Again, length supplies a useful example. Earlier I characterised $\circ$ on $\mathbf{L}$ in terms of laying objects end-to-end. However, there are other ways of concatenating lengths that we might have employed as primitives instead. One alternative (also discussed by Ellis 1968, 80–1) is *right-angled concatenation*. Say that $L \odot L' = L''$ just when L'' is the length of the hypotenuse of the right-angled triangle with catheti of lengths L and L'. (See Figure 3; I did have to look that word up.) *Right-angled concatenation* has all the same key properties as *end-to-end concatenation* which permit additive measurement. In an alternative history, then, we might have chosen to measure length by mapping $\langle \mathbf{L}, \gtrsim; \odot \rangle$ into $\langle \mathbb{R}^{\geq 0}, \geq; + \rangle$. (Or $\langle \mathbb{R}^{\geq 1}, \geq; \times \rangle$, or $\langle \mathbb{R}, \geq; * \rangle$, or …) This would have simplified how we express the relationships between sides of a right-angled triangle, though it would also have made calculating end-to-end concatenations of distances slightly more difficult.

With that said, I don't want to give the impression that anything goes. A minimal constraint on the choice of qualitative system is that the primitives must be *natural*. Without some such constraint, we trivialise the whole endeavour. For instance, assuming no more than that $\mathbf{L}$ can be mapped into $\mathbb{R}$, we know

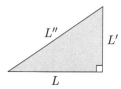

Figure 3 L'' is the right-angled concatenation of L and L' (i.e., $L \odot L' = L''$).

already that there exists a binary relation R on $\mathbf{L}$ that maps into $\geq$, in the sense that

$$(L, L') \in R \text{ if and only if } \varphi(L) \geq \varphi(L').$$

Likewise, supposing only that $\langle \mathbf{L}, \succsim \rangle$ maps into $\langle \mathbb{R}, \geq \rangle$, we know already that there will exist at least one ternary relation R such that

$$(L, L', L'') \in R \text{ if and only if } \varphi(L) + \varphi(L') = \varphi(L'').$$

So the fact that we can then find *some* relations on $\mathbf{L}$ corresponding to $\geq$ and $+$ is thoroughly uninteresting. We can derive such relations from *any* mapping of $\mathbf{L}$ into $\mathbb{R}$, so long as we're permissive enough about what counts as a relation. It's a matter of convention what we take the primitive relations in our qualitative systems to be, that is true, but measurement is only *interesting* when those relations are *natural*.

2.5 Meaningfulness

A focus of the discussion to follow involves differentiating what is meaningful from what is not in the measurement of belief. The most common strategy for drawing such distinctions goes via *invariance*. Essentially, the idea is that a numerical property or relation is meaningful only if it's invariant across alternative numerical representations; otherwise, it's a mere artefact of convention.

Compare the case of temperature. When represented in °C, water freezes at 0 and boils at 100, the hottest temperature recorded in Australia is almost exactly half way between these values (50.7) and more than double the hottest temperature recorded in Antarctica (19.8). But not all of the numerical properties and relations just mentioned are *meaningful*. Measured in °F, water freezes at 32 and boils at 212, the hottest recorded temperature in Australia (123) is less than twice the hottest temperature in Antarctica (68), though it'll still be just over halfway between the freezing and boiling points of water. Celsius and Fahrenheit are equally legitimate interval scale measures of temperature – they're *numerically* distinct but they're not *meaningfully* distinct. The particular values associated with each temperature and the ratios between those values vary between alternative scales, and they are therefore not meaningful. Ratios of differences are invariant, on the other hand, and so we call them meaningful.

So far, so good. But consider again the additive measures of $\langle \mathbf{L}, \gtrsim; \circ \rangle$. If φ and ψ are any two additive measures of that system, then

$$\varphi(L) = 2\varphi(L') \text{ if and only if } \psi(L) = 2\psi(L').$$

But this, too, is an artefact of conventions – in the choice of numerical system. As we've just discussed, the *qualitative* relation that holds between L and L' whenever L' is *twice as long* as L isn't *itself* a ratio relation in any deep sense, and if θ is a multiplicative measure of length, then

$$\varphi(L) = 2\varphi(L') \text{ if and only if } \theta(L) = \theta(L')^2.$$

In that broader sense, almost all the information in *any* numerical representation of $\langle \mathbf{L}, \gtrsim; \circ \rangle$ is an artefact of convention. There's approximately nothing that's invariant across *all* numerical representations of a qualitative system, and what *is* preserved is far too little to be of much interest.

The upshot is that meaningfulness needs to be understood relative to a fixed choice of numerical system. A more precise account of meaningfulness, and one that incorporates this lesson, originates with Pfanzagl (1968). I present it here in lightly modified form:

Definition 6. Suppose that $\Phi(Q, \mathcal{N})$ is non-empty, where $Q = \langle \mathbf{X}, R_i; \bullet_j \rangle$ and $\mathcal{N} = \langle \mathbf{Y}, S_i; *_j \rangle$. For any $\varphi \in \Phi(Q, \mathcal{N})$ and any n-ary relation S on $\mathbf{Y}$, $R(S, \varphi)$ is the *relation induced on* $\mathbf{X}$ *by* S *and* φ if and only if

$$(x_1, \ldots, x_n) \in R(S, \varphi) \text{ if and only if } (\varphi(x_1), \ldots, \varphi(x_n)) \in S.$$

S is *Q-meaningful relative to* $\mathcal{N}$ when $R(S, \varphi)$ doesn't depend on the choice of φ in $\Phi(Q, \mathcal{N})$.

Where the Q and $\mathcal{N}$ are obvious given context, we simply say that S is meaningful. Note one: if S is among the primitive *relations* S_i of $\mathcal{N}$, then $R(S, \varphi)$ is just the corresponding primitive relation R_i in Q and thus $R(S, \varphi)$ is automatically Q-meaningful relative to $\mathcal{N}$. So we're only interested in the case where S *isn't* among the primitives relations of $\mathcal{N}$. Note two: if S is one of the primitive *operations* of $\mathcal{N}$, then it *doesn't* automatically follow that S is meaningful, except in the special case where every homomorphism in $\Phi(Q, \mathcal{N})$ is a strong homomorphism. So being a primitive *relation* in $\mathcal{N}$ suffices for being meaningful, being a primitive *operation* doesn't.

To get a grip on Definition 6, it's helpful to compare cases where a numerical relation isn't meaningful. Observe first of all that *every* numerical property or relation S induces a corresponding property or relation $R(S, \varphi)$ on the qualitative system relative to each $\varphi \in \Phi(Q, N)$. So, if some ordinal scale φ maps $Q = \langle \mathbf{L}, \gtrsim \rangle$ into $N = \langle \mathbb{R}, \geq \rangle$, the 2:1 ratio relation induces a corresponding relation on $\mathbf{L}$ that holds for L, L' whenever $\varphi(L) = 2\varphi(L')$. But that relation isn't Q-meaningful relative to N, precisely because $R(2{:}1, \varphi)$ needn't equal $R(2{:}1, \psi)$ for every other ψ in $\Phi(Q, N)$. By contrast, the 2:1 ratio *is* meaningful relative to the additive measures of $\langle \mathbf{L}, \gtrsim; \circ \rangle$, since $R(2{:}1, \varphi)$ equals $R(2{:}1, \psi)$ for any two additive measures φ and ψ. (Why does that matter? Because if the 2:1 ratio is meaningful with respect to the additive measurement of length, then we can draw generalisations and formulate laws involving that ratio without worrying that it all depends on an arbitrary choice of scale.)

In general, the idea is that a numerical relation is meaningful inasmuch as it always corresponds to the same qualitative relation regardless of what homo-morphism we care to use, given a fixed choice of numerical system. That's just what 'meaningful' *means* in this context: *always picks out the same thing inde-pendent of the choice of scale*. So to make some headway on the matter of what should be considered meaningful in our numerical representations of belief, we need to say more about the kinds of qualitative structures these representations are supposed to be representations of.

3 Clarifications and Desiderata

The central questions to be addressed by an account of the measurement of belief are, in relation to a given purported numerical representation of belief: (i) what is the qualitative system being represented, (ii) what is the numerical system in which it's represented, and (iii) under what conditions are such rep-resentations possible? Answer these, and you'll have a complete theory of the measurement of belief; don't answer them, and all you'll have are numbers.

An epistemic approach, I said, is one that explains the measurement of belief by appeal to the internal structure of the belief system. Better: an epistemic approach is one according to which the qualitative system being represented can be characterised fully in terms of doxastic states and the relations between them, where a *doxastic state* is any type of mental state with a belief-*ish* flavour. This might include states of all-or-nothing belief, levels of confidence, judge-ments of comparative probability, judgements of when one thing is evidence for another thing or when they are independent, and so on. In sum, doxastic states are the sorts of mental states that have a mind-to-world direction of fit, broadly construed; or the sorts of things that reflect our opinions regarding what the world is like and what it might be like, and that ought to be responsive to evidence independent of our preferences. Epistemic approaches are covered in Section 4 and Section 5.

Decision-theoretic approaches appeal instead to relations between doxastic states and conative states (read: states with a desire-*ish* flavour) to explain what the numbers mean. Roughly, a paradigmatic decision-theoretic approach is one where the qualitative system is comprised of a conjoint system of beliefs and basic desires (as opposed to derivative or instrumental desires), related via their joint determination of a preference ordering over a space of actions according to some decision rule; the numerical representation of the preference relation is then constructed to capture the systematic relations holding between the three. Decision-theoretic approaches are covered in Section 6.

But before we delve into the details, this section provides some background clarifications on what a theory of belief measurement is and what it is not (section 3.1 and section 3.2), followed by some simplifying assumptions (section 3.3) and general desiderata (section 3.4) that will be relevant to the discussion throughout.

3.1 Quantitation, Not Elicitation

In the classic presentations of the RTM, qualitative systems are understood to be *empirical relational systems*. These systems are built around primitives that are directly and publicly observable in the context of some experimental procedure. For example, rather than characterising the length system $\langle \mathbf{L}, \succsim; \circ \rangle$ as a set of attributes and higher-order relations between them, if I were doing things in the classical manner, then I'd have characterised it as a set of rigid physical objects, the observable *at least as long* relation between them, and a concatenation operation interpreted as the physical process of taking two rigid objects and joining them to form a new composite object. Essentially, empirical relational systems are systems in which nothing is hidden from view – the relations should be open to observation, the relata should be things we can touch and see and poke and prod, and the operations are physical procedures on or processes observed in the entities being measured.

There are some obvious problems that arise when measurement is understood this way. (These problems were not unknown to the founders of the representational theory; cf. Krantz *et al.* 1971, 27–31.) In violation of ubiquitous transitivity axioms, for example, one might have a series of objects each longer than the preceding by an imperceptible amount, such that adjacent objects will be observed to be of the same length even while the last is much longer than the first. Similar problems arise for all empirical relational systems, and will be familiar from the history of operationalism. They all point to the same basic issue: quantities cannot be perfectly characterised in terms of the experimental procedures by which they're measured, since no such procedure is ever perfect. Instead, measurement procedures are developed on the basis of what our best theories imply about the conditions under which observable experimental outcomes will reliably (albeit imperfectly) correlate with variations in some limited range of magnitudes of the quantity we desire to measure.[8]

But it would be a mistake to dismiss the classical RTM focus on empirical relational systems as mere offshoots of some outdated operationalism. Much more illuminating to say that the mathematical framework of the theory was built to play two separable explanatory roles. On the one hand, it's there to explain how we might use numerical properties and relations to represent and reason about bits of the world that aren't themselves numerical in nature. That explanation appeals to structure-preserving mappings between qualitative and numerical systems, and matters of *observability* are irrelevant here. On the other hand, the very same formalisms were supposed to help guide the design of actual measurement procedures. The empirical relational system for the measurement of length, for instance, was supposed to be formulated in such a way that it might feasibly be implemented in some empirical procedure for measuring lengths – hence the pervasiveness of error in all realistic measurement practices was taken to present a serious problem for the RTM (cf. Krantz *et al.* 1971, 1–9, 25, 27–31).

We can – and should – keep these roles separate. The RTM is great for the first, not so great for the second.[9] As Kyburg (1984) once said, the 'theory of measurement is difficult enough without bringing in the theory of making measurements' (p. 7). Unfortunately, ambiguity in how we use the term 'measurement' can obscure this point. Compare the 'measurement of mass' qua abstract pairing of determinate mass attributes with numbers, such that relations between the latter usefully mirror relations between the former; versus the 'measurement of mass' qua empirical procedure for determining the mass of particular objects by means of an equal-armed pan balance. The original intention was that the RTM will be a theory of both – and the sad result has been that it's routinely criticised for being of little relevance to the actual measurement

---

[8] See Mari et al. (2017) for relevant discussion, plus a detailed account of the theory-based construction of one such procedure for the measurement of the mass of stars.

[9] This opinion is neither new nor uncommon; similar can be found expressed in Roberts (1985), Mundy (1987; 1994), Swoyer (1991), Narens and Luce (1993), Decoene *et al.* (1995), Mari *et al.* (2017), and Baccelli (2020). See also Michell (2021) for a useful overview of the history of thinking on this matter.

practices of working scientists (e.g., Borsboom 2005; Mari 2005; Reiss 2016). Such criticisms lack bite when we recognise that the RTM was always better understood as a framework for understanding meaning and meaningfulness in our numerical representations of systems of determinable attributes as posited by a scientific theory.

In light this, let me emphasise firmly that a theory of belief measurement *as presently understood* is not in the business of explaining how we might gather empirical evidence as to the strength of an agent's beliefs through the observation of their behaviour, nor how we might elicit their beliefs by any other means. Mario Bunge (1973) once recommended avoiding the ambiguity of 'measurement' by referring to the abstract sense as *quantitation.* The terminological suggestion never much caught on, but in those terms our topic is the quantitation of beliefs rather than their elicitation.

Consequently, I also suggest we make no presumptions regarding the observability of the qualitative primitives posited within a theory of belief measurement. These systems posit psychological relations – things like *is more confident than, is more desirable than, is indifferent between* – and it would be an error to presume that such relations will be directly observable in behaviour.[10] It would be a deeper error still to assume that these relations *must* be observable, if we're to justify theses about the structure of the qualitative systems involving them. Quantities are posits of our scientific theories, and like any other posits they need not be directly observable. The justification for the hypothesis that a qualitative system has a certain formal structure that permits a certain format of numerical representation need not derive from any direct observations of that structure, but can instead derive indirectly from the broader empirical and theoretical virtues of the theories that presuppose a system of quantities endowed with that structure. In this respect the measurement of belief is no different in kind than the measurement of any other quantity.

3.2 Measurement, Not Metaphysics

This is an work on measurement, not metaphysics. Experience teaches that these can be hard to keep separate, but separate them we should – lest we end up rejecting perfectly reasonable approaches to the measurement of belief by mixing them up with hideously implausible views on the metaphysics of belief.

---

[10] *Perhaps*, under special circumstances, I'd agree that a limited part of a person's overall preference ordering might be 'directly revealed' through their choice behaviour alone. Many people have thought so. But even given all the hedging, I'm still doubtful. At best, there's a defeasible evidential relationship between choice and preference, and the connection between them is too loose to say that preferences are ever *directly* observable via choices.

The core questions dealt with by a theory of belief measurement concern the specific matter of quantitation: in relation to a purported numerical representation of some doxastic state or set of such states,

1. what is the qualitative system Q being represented,
2. what is the numerical system N in which it's represented, and
3. under what conditions are such representations possible?

By contrast, a metaphysics of belief is concerned with much broader questions about the kinds of ontological and/or conceptual dependence relations that hold between doxastic states of different kinds, and between doxastic states and the wider world.[11] The core task of such a metaphysics is, in short, to explain what kinds of doxastic state-types there are, and where they ought to be situated relative to one another and relative to the rest of the world within some general conceptual framework and/or global ontology of the universe.

One major division in the metaphysics of belief is between *realist* and *anti-realist* views. Broadly speaking, the former says that the correct attribution of a doxastic state to an agent depends on objective facts about the agent, and the latter says that correct attribution depends somehow on who's doing the attributing. Some versions of *interpretivism* fall into the anti-realist camp; such will typically say that an agent's beliefs are just those an interpreter can usefully employ to explain the agent's behaviour. Among realists, a major division is between *representational* and *non-representational* theories. The former explains what it is to have a doxastic state with such-and-such content by hypothesising the existence of some internal mental representation of that content. Non-representational theories link doxastic states instead to not-necessarily-representational states of the agent that are systematically related to the contents thereof. Among non-representational views are *behaviourist* theories, which analyse doxastic states as patterns of behaviour; *dispositionalist* theories, which analyse doxastic states via a suite of associated (and not-necessarily-behavioural) dispositions; and *functionalist* theories, which analyse doxastic states by reference to a functional role that typically revolves around relations between beliefs over time given evidence and between beliefs, desires and behaviour.

---

[11] It's not easy to say precisely what dependence relations are, and any characterisation I give will be subject to debate. Roughly, a concept C is *conceptually* more fundamental than another concept C' when C' can be analysed in terms of C but not vice versa; and a property (or state-type) P is *ontologically* more fundamental than another P' when the instantiation of P' necessarily depends on the instantiation of P but not vice versa. Another way to distinguish the two is via their explanatory roles: ontological dependence explains necessary connections between properties, while conceptual dependence explains a priori connections between propositions.

While there are some connections between measurement and metaphysics – some ways of approaching the former will fit more or less naturally with different ways of approaching the latter – in general, one cannot read metaphysics off of measurement. Every epistemic and decision-theoretic approach to the measurement of belief that's considered in the following sections is compatible with a wide range of views on the metaphysics of belief – including all of those just mentioned. There's nothing intrinsically *realist* or *anti-realist*, or *representationalist* or *non-representationalist*, or *behaviourist* or *dispositionalist* or *functionalist* (and so on) about any of these measurement theories.

This point is especially worth emphasising in the case of decision-theoretic accounts of belief measurement. Historically there has been a close connection between the decision-theoretic representation theorems that underlie those accounts, and behaviourist (or behaviourist-lite) metaphysical theories which propose to reduce beliefs to preferences as revealed by choices. Since this kind of behaviourism is nowadays treated like a bad smell, decision-theoretic approaches to the measurement of belief seem to have been tainted by association and are thereby often dismissed without much consideration. So I want to consider that case in a bit more detail, as on reflection there's not much reason to link the decision-theoretic approaches specifically to behaviourism.

A typical decision-theoretic representation theorem establishes sufficient conditions for the conjoint measurement of beliefs, desires, and preferences. The general idea is that an agent's preference ordering will be determined by their beliefs and desires via some decision rule (e.g., expected utility maximisation), and so we want to construct a numerical representation of those preferences which 'decomposes' into independent representations of belief and desire via that decision rule. (Compare the example in section 2.3, with the representation of **C** 'decomposing' into representations of its determinants **A** and **B** via some rule f.) These theorems don't tell us anything about the metaphysical relationship between beliefs, desires, and preferences. Consider: if I describe a structure for the conjoint measurement of momentum as determined by mass and velocity, then no one leaps to the conclusion that mass and velocity are ontologically dependent on momentum. Likewise, if I describe a structure for the conjoint measurement of discomfort as determined by temperature and humidity, no one infers that the concepts of *temperature* and *humidity* ought to be analysed in terms of *discomfort*. Such inferences would be *obviously* fallacious – so why would we draw parallel inferences from decision-theoretic representation theorems?

According to the decision-theoretic approach, the conjoint representation is supposed to capture a systematic relation or relations between beliefs, desires, and preferences that is *explanatorily relevant to the quantitation of belief.* Nothing about this implies that beliefs depend conceptually or onto-logically on preferences. Moreover, the explanatorily relevant relations may not be dependence relations at all. For example, the approach would be con-sistent with a functionalist metaphysics according to which beliefs, desires and preferences are interrelated posits in a psychological theory such that none are reducible to the others, and such that their statistically or biologic-ally normal causal interactions can be systematically represented within a decision-theoretic framework.

Observe, also, that such a functionalist might say the relation between beliefs and preferences is critical for explaining the quantitation of belief, even while saying that the characteristic functional role of belief isn't *exhausted* by those relations. One might suppose that an important part of the functional role of belief concerns the connection between beliefs and sensory evidence – a state cannot rightly be said to 'play the belief-role' if it isn't appropriately sensitive to perceived changes in the environment. Such relationships will be crucial when providing a functionalist *analysis of what beliefs are*, but that doesn't imply they need also be mentioned in an *explanation of why it makes sense to represent a system of beliefs within a certain numerical framework*. These are related issues, to be sure, but nevertheless clearly distinct.

Compare the case of mass. Our concept of *mass* can be plausibly analysed in terms of its theoretical role: mass is the property that best satisfies the total role associated with 'mass' within contemporary physics. But mass does many things. The mass of an object is proportionate to its resistance to acceleration as measured by an observer at rest with respect to it. It's also proportionate to the strength of the gravitational field the object exerts on others, and its total rest energy. Mass is tied to momentum and velocity, density and volume, and to how fast a transverse wave travels through a string attached to a fixed point at each end. Mass also plays a role in stellar evolution; for instance, a white dwarf with mass exceeding about 1.4 solar masses will succumb to electron degeneracy pressure and collapse into either a neutron star or a black hole. So if you want to analyse *mass* by reference to its total theoretical role, then there's a lot you need to mention – but if you just want to give an explanation of why it makes sense to measure mass on a ratio scale, then not all of that is going to be necessary or relevant. In sum: the relations we use to *analyse the concept* of a quantity can come apart from the typically narrower class of relations we use to *explain the quantitation* of that quantity.

An account of the measurement of belief just isn't in the business of explain-ing ontological or conceptual dependence relations that hold between different kinds of doxastic states, nor between doxastic states and non-doxastic states. It would be wise, then, to be very careful when drawing metaphysical conclusions from measurement-theoretic premises.

3.3 Simplifying Assumptions

Having said some things about the sorts of things we shouldn't be assuming, let me now talk about the things I will be assuming. There are three assumptions in total; the first two are simplifying assumptions about how we model contents:

Assumption 1 Degrees of belief have propositional contents, where propositions can be modelled as subsets of some non-empty space of possible worlds (henceforth denoted Ω).

Assumption 2 For each agent and all propositions p, there exists an algebra of propositions $\mathcal{A}$ on Ω such that the agent has some degree of belief towards p if and only if p belongs to $\mathcal{A}$.

By 'possible', I mean at least consistent with classical logic. An algebra of propositions is defined like so:

Definition 7. $\mathcal{A}$ is an *algebra of propositions* on Ω if and only if it is a non-empty set of subsets of Ω, and for all $p, q \subseteq \Omega$,

1. If p is in $\mathcal{A}$, then $\Omega \setminus p$ (henceforth $\neg p$) is in $\mathcal{A}$
2. If p and q are in $\mathcal{A}$, then $p \cup q$ is in $\mathcal{A}$

Furthermore, an element $a \in \mathcal{A}$ is an *atom* of the algebra if and only if $a \neq \varnothing$ and for every $p \in \mathcal{A}$, either $a \cap p = a$ or $a \cap p = \varnothing$.

These are substantive assumptions indeed, and I'm not super confident they're true – but they're also both very standard assumptions in the present context, and each does a great deal to help simplify many matters.[12]

Still, I should say a bit more about these two assumptions, since they'll play an important role at some points of the discussion. An immediate consequence of **Assumption 1** is that the contents of belief are *coarse-grained*: if p and q are logically equivalent, then $p = q$. But I did not call it a 'simplifying' assumption due to this fact – there's a lot to be said in favour of coarse-grained content! (e.g., Stalnaker 1984; Lewis 1986; Chalmers 2011.) Rather, I consider **Assumption 1** to be a simplifying assumption because it (in effect) has

---

[12] Also for the sake of simplicity, I will mostly focus on measurement structures involving finite algebras. This is not because I think that agents can have degrees of belief towards only finitely many propositions, but just because trying to cover both the finite and infinite cases would add significant complexity with comparatively little by way of philosophical pay-off.

us ignore so-called *de se* content and certain common strategies for the representation thereof that require going a little ways beyond the standard possible worlds framework (e.g., Lewis 1979).

Opponents of coarse-grained content often suppose we can model more fine-grained contents using impossible worlds. Roughly, the idea is that wherever we want to differentiate between logically equivalent contents p and q, we can include in our space of worlds Ω one or more impossible worlds where one of these holds but the other doesn't; hence the set of p-worlds will come apart from the set of q-worlds. But matters are not quite so easy. One cannot simply throw a bunch of impossible worlds into Ω without potentially breaking something elsewhere, especially in the presence of **Assumption 2**.

To explain why, it'll help to have a specific account of what impossible worlds are and how they're used to model contents. For the purposes of the discussion I'll adopt the modal ersatz approach found in Nolan (1997), though essentially the same points can be made for other popular accounts of impossible worlds (e.g., linguistic ersatzism or extended modal realism, see Elliott 2019b for discussion). Following Nolan's preferred terminology, take *propositions* – the potential objects of our beliefs and the meanings of our declarative sentences, whatever they may be – to be ontological primitives. Given that, we let a world ω be any set of propositions, and we say that p is true at a world ω just in case $p \in \omega$. There is, of course, a one-to-one correspondence between each primitive proposition p and the set of worlds containing p (the p-worlds). We say a world is possible just in case it's *complete* (contains either p or its negation, for every proposition p) and *consistent* (has no logically inconsistent subsets); otherwise, it's impossible. If Ω contains only possible worlds, then if p logically implies q then every p-world in Ω will be a q-world. But if Ω isn't restricted to possible worlds, then it may be that p implies q even while there are some impossible p-worlds in Ω that aren't q-worlds. Much therefore depends on what kinds of worlds get to go into Ω; the richer the space of worlds, the more distinctions we can draw between logically-equivalent contents modelled as sets of worlds.

Impossible worlds theorists will often assume a very rich space of worlds characterised by an *unrestricted comprehension* principle: for any complete set of primitive propositions $\mathcal{P} = \{p, q, \ldots\}$, there is a world $\omega \in \Omega$ such that $\omega = \mathcal{P}$. Roughly, for any possibility or impossibility, there's a world that verifies it; and the principle thereby ensures there are always some p-worlds that aren't q-worlds even when p logically implies q. However, unrestricted comprehension also has the consequence that many subsets of Ω are *meaningless*. These are sets of worlds that correspond to no primitive proposition whatever, and so are not fit (by hypothesis) to serve as the objects of belief. There is nothing that's true at all and only the worlds in a meaningless set – they are just artefacts of the construction of contents as sets of sets of primitive propositions. For example, and as Nolan (1997, 563) points out, any set containing only *possible* worlds will be meaningless in this sense given unrestricted comprehension. For any set of possible worlds $\{\omega_1, \omega_2, \ldots\}$ there will be some propositions they all have in common. Given that, let ω_i be a world such that everything true at all the worlds in $\{\omega_1, \omega_2, \ldots\}$ is also true at ω_i, but the negation of one or more of those things is also true at ω_i. It follows that ω_i is an impossible world. So, there is nothing true at all *and only* a set of possible worlds – such sets are meaningless.

The existence of meaningless subsets of Ω isn't intrinsically problematic. However, it does not play nicely with **Assumption 2**. An algebra of propositions is closed under relative complements and binary unions, and in the presence of *unrestricted comprehension* two facts follow. First, the relative complement of any meaningful proposition is meaningless: for any p and q there will be impossible worlds where both p and q hold, hence there's no q such that the set of p-worlds doesn't intersect with the set of q-worlds. Second, the union of any two meaningful propositions is meaningless: for any p and q there can be no r such that the set of r-worlds is the union of the p-worlds and the q-worlds, since then every p-world would be an r-world but for any p and r there will be some p-worlds that aren't r-worlds. In short, then: any algebra of propositions defined on a sufficiently rich space of possible and impossible worlds will consist *mostly* of meaningless sets – and we shouldn't want to represent agents as having beliefs towards entities that correspond to no proper object of belief.

You might think there's an easy response: the main premises of the foregoing reasoning are *unrestricted comprehension* and **Assumption 2**, so we can simply deny one or both of those and avoid the problem – right? Again, though, matters aren't so simple. For one thing, *unrestricted comprehension* or something in the nearby vicinity is required for the most attractive results that impossible worlds are advertised to have in relation to fine-grained content and logical omniscience (see Nolan 2013 for an overview). But moreover, it's a mistake to suppose that *unrestricted comprehension* is necessary for the conclusion – as if the problem would simply disappear were we to adopt a more restricted principle. As shown in Elliott (2019b), the real problem is that **Assumption 2** imposes a Boolean algebraic structure over meaningful subsets of Ω, which forces the worlds in Ω to conform to a Boolean logic. Under quite minimal richness conditions on what kinds of *possible* worlds go into Ω, either (a) every algebra of sets on Ω will contain meaningless sets of worlds or (b) the worlds in Ω will be closed under the $\{\neg, \wedge\}$-fragment of Boolean logic (or something to the same effect).

Nor is it easy to deny **Assumption 2** since – as we'll see – many theories for the measurement of belief make important use of that assumption. This includes all of the epistemic approaches that I will discuss in what follows, and a large number of decision-theoretic approaches too. The reason why the assumption is important ultimately boils down to the fact that representation of any quantity on anything stronger than an ordinal scale requires a qualitative structure richer than what can be provided by a single weak ordering over the magnitudes thereof – basically, some additional relation will be required for the extra-ordinal structure of the numerical representation to grock on to. Thus, in the measurement of length we require not only the *at least as long* relation, but also a concatenation operation that can be mapped into addition. Likewise for conjoint measurement, where the additional structure is supplied by reconstructing $\gtrsim$ on the single quantity **C** as a quarternary relation over **A**×**B** and then using induced relations between the factors **A** and **B** to supply the additional structure for the representation. For theories of belief measurement, the additional structure that allows for the possibility of more-than-merely-ordinal measurement is often characterised by set-theoretic relations between contents (qua sets of worlds) in such a way that presupposes the algebraic structure guaranteed by **Assumption 2**.

The point here is *not* that there's no hope for impossible worlds, or that we shouldn't make use of them. Rather, the point is that incorporating impossible worlds into contemporary theories of belief measurement will require careful consideration about the nature of content and likely some further adjustments to our formal models and their interpretation. The common thought among many philosophers is that impossible worlds present an *easy fix* to the problems of coarse-grained content – just throw some impossible worlds into Ω and you're done. But it is not so easy. In that sense, then, the conjunction of **Assumption 1** and **Assumption 2** can be considered a simplifying assumption as well.

One more simplifying assumption:

Assumption 3 Degrees of belief are precise.

I don't think this assumption is realistic. Imagine, for instance, that a downtrodden magician has just rolled into town. He has a coin, which you happen to know is biased but you know not in what direction the bias lies nor to what degree. He also has an old deck of cards with some unspecified number of cards missing. The magician tosses the coin and pulls out a single card from the deck. Let p be the proposition that *the coin lands heads*, and q that *the card is red*. If degrees of belief are precise (represented by real values), and you have some positive degree of confidence in each of p and q, then there must be some precise value n such that you're exactly n times as confident in p as you are in q. Plausibly, though, there is no such n, or at least there needn't be.

Over the past few decades, something of a consensus has emerged regarding the representation of 'imprecise' degrees of belief (see, e.g., Walley 1991; Kaplan 2010; Joyce 2010). Instead of the real-valued functions employed in classical models of graded belief, we use a set of real-valued functions – a *credal set*, or as it's often known in philosophy, a *representor*. The rough idea is that what a representor represents is what's true according to all functions in the set. Thus, for example, we say the subject has at least as much confidence in p as she does in q just when every function in her representor assigns a value to p that's at least as great as the value assigned to q. Moreover, a general strategy exists for the construction of these 'representor' representations that can be applied to the different epistemic and decision-theoretic approaches discussed in what follows (e.g., Evren & Ok 2011; Alon & Lehrer 2014; Alon & Schmeidler 2014; Augustin *et al.* 2014; Hawthorne 2016). The main move is to replace the common *weak order* axiom that's used to construct a precise real-valued representation with a strictly weaker *preorder* axiom, thus allowing for incompleteness in the primitive psychological relations being represented. The 'imprecise' representation is then constructed from the many precise representations of the various possible completions of that preorder.

Since this is a general strategy that works more or less the same way across epistemic and decision-theoretic approaches, I've neglected to include details. Instead, I'll take it as read that the real-valued measures of belief considered in what follows are idealisations – and relatively harmless idealisations, in that we have a good sense of how to do away with them. (See also section 6.4 for a little more discussion on this.)

3.4 Desiderata

The remainder of this section will outline four desiderata for a theory of belief measurement. To be clear: I will not be explicitly evaluating the theories of belief measurement by reference to these desiderata. Evaluation is left to the reader, and you may take issue with some (or all) of what I take to be theoretically desirable. Rather, the desiderata are here offered by way of explanation for why I've chosen to focus on certain topics in the chapters that follow – namely the meaningfulness of extra-ordinal information, probabilistic and non-probabilistic representations, and logical omniscience.

Again I'll need to start with some terminology. We take a probability measure to be defined as follows:

Definition 8. Where $\mathcal{A}$ is an algebra of propositions on Ω, $\mu\colon \mathcal{A} \mapsto \mathbb{R}$ is a *probability measure* if and only if, for all $p, q \in \mathcal{A}$,

1. $\mu(p) \geq 0$ (*non-negativity*)
2. $\mu(\Omega) = 1$ (*normalisation*)
3. If $p \cap q = \varnothing$, then $\mu(p \cup q) = \mu(p) + \mu(q)$ ($\sqcup$-*additivity*)

According to *probabilism*, ideally rational agents are those whose beliefs can be accurately represented by some probability measure. Now, exactly *what it is* for a system of beliefs to be represented by a probability measure is a question to be settled by an account of the measurement of belief – so probabilism is a thesis that only makes sense against the backdrop of some measurement theory. But set that aside. A weaker version of the thesis, what Kaplan (2010) calls *modest probabilism*, requires that an ideally rational system of beliefs can be represented by a non-empty set of probability measures.

I want something even weaker: at least some rational systems of belief are represented by (sets of) probability measures. Call it *really modest probabilism*. While there are occasional arguments against (modest) probabilism, these usually highlight surprising exceptions to the thesis that ideally rational agents must *always* be represented by (sets of) probability measures. So I take it that really modest probabilism will be generally uncontroversial, and as such we should desire a theory of belief measurement that's in a position to make sense of it:

Desideratum 1 A theory of the measurement of belief should be consistent really modest probabilism.

That is, the theory should be able to explain how a system of beliefs *might* be accurately represented by some probability measure (or a set thereof).[13]

For the next, let's say that a measure of belief is *cardinal* (as opposed to *merely ordinal*) if it's unique up to something stronger than an order-preserving transformation. So, for example, interval-scale and ratio-scale measures will count as cardinal measures in this sense. Given that,

Desideratum 2 Probabilistic representations of belief are (at least in some theoretical contexts) cardinal measures of those beliefs.

---

[13] Given this is what the vast majority of epistemic and decision-theoretic approaches in fact do, I don't expect much resistance on this front. Still, **Desideratum 1** plays a non-trivial role in constraining what counts as a desirable theory of belief measurement, especially when combined with the remaining desiderata. This will be more apparent in Section 4.2.

One reason to accept this desideratum is intuition. Most will be happy to say that a rational agent ought to have about 50 per cent confidence that a fair coin will land heads on a single toss, which should be *half as much* confidence as they have regarding it landing either heads or tails, and *twice as much* confidence as they ought to have regarding it landing heads twice in a row. Or, more straightforwardly, it's clearly sensible to say that a person can have *much more* confidence in one thing than in another. Such claims makes sense only if beliefs are measurable on something stronger than an ordinal scale.

I'm inclined to take these intuitions seriously, as indicative of how we pre-theoretically (and post-theoretically) tend to think about confidence. But I wouldn't want to rest my case on such intuitions alone. A stronger reason to accept **Desideratum 2** arises from the fact that more-than-merely-ordinal information has a theoretical role to play in our standard (and non-standard) theories of rational decision-making. Consider the following example. We imagine first that Ramsey has to choose between two gambles:

α: receive \$1 if p is true, nothing otherwise
β: receive \$2 if p is false, nothing otherwise

Suppose also that Ramsey considers p less probable than Ω but more probable than $\neg p$. Without loss of generality, let the algebra $\mathcal{A}$ be $\{\Omega, p, \neg p, \varnothing\}$. A probability measure will be a merely ordinal representation of Ramsey's confidences just in case it assigns a value to p that's strictly between 1 and $\frac{1}{2}$. As such, there's at least two ordinally equivalent probability measures, μ_1 and μ_2, such that

$$1 > \mu_1(p) > \frac{2}{3}, \qquad \frac{2}{3} > \mu_2(p) > \frac{1}{2}.$$

If confidence is measured on nothing stronger than an ordinal scale, then there should be no difference in *meaning* between μ_1 and μ_2. But according to expected utility theory, there *is* a difference: Ramsey should prefer α if and only if his confidence in p is more than twice his confidence in $\neg p$. At that point, the higher probability of winning with α outweighs the promise of a larger prize with β. So expected utility theory is inconsistent with the thesis that confidence is measured on a merely ordinal scale. (I'll say more about this in Section 6.3.)

The same holds for most alternatives to expected utility theory, including normative theories (for representing ideally rational agents) and descriptive theories (for representing realistic agents). And we needn't rest the case on decision-theoretic examples either. Much the same holds in contemporary epistemology, where a great deal of theory and argument presumes the more-than-merely-ordinal measurement of belief. Two brief examples; I'm sure if you start looking you'll find more. First, the relation of probabilistic independence is crucially important for Bayesian theories of evidence and learning, but independence relations can vary between ordinally equivalent numerical representations (see Section 5.3). Second, epistemic utility theory appeals to numerical properties that differentiate ordinally equivalent probability measures (see Mayo-Wilson & Wheeler 2019, p. 19). In sum: if our numerical representations of belief are to play the roles that they are in fact generally taken to play in contemporary theories of rational belief and rational decision-making, then they cannot be mere ordinal-scale measures. That's not a conclusive reason for accepting **Desideratum 2**, of course, but it *is* a reason, and a potent one.

Together, **Desideratum 1** and **Desideratum 2** imply that at least some possible agents have beliefs that are representable by a probability measure, where that probability measure isn't merely an ordinal scale. But for all that's said, it may be that cardinal measurement is only possible in the special case of ideally rational agents – everyone else is stuck with mere ordinal measures. The next desideratum is aimed at denying this. Say that an agent is *logically omniscient* just in case, if p logically entails q, then the agent has no more confidence in p than they do in q. In other words, their confidences are ordered coherently with respect to logical implication. Then:

Desideratum 3 Logical omniscience is not a prerequisite for the cardinal measurement of belief.

The argument I'll provide for **Desideratum 3** *is* just based on intuition. I'm not ideally rational, and neither are you. We are less-than-ideally rational, and one likely manifestation of this fact is that we aren't logically omniscient. But this doesn't prevent us from believing one proposition *much more* than another, or *about half as much* as another, and so on. (If there are any Moorean facts in the theory of belief measurement, this ought to be one of them.) Furthermore, given **Assumption 1**, any probabilistic representation of beliefs will automatically determine a logically omniscient confidence ordering. So, consequence: probabilistic representation is not a prerequisite for cardinal representation either.

The joint effect of the three desiderata so far will be that we should want a theory of how beliefs can be measured on something stronger than an ordinal scale, which is *consistent* with really modest probabilism but isn't *limited* to representing the beliefs of the logically omniscient. We want a theory of cardinal belief measurement for ideal and non-ideal agents. The final desideratum is an anti-disjunctiveness condition:

Desideratum 4 A theory of belief measurement should not be fundamentally different for ideal versus non-ideal agents.

If we're going to say that both ideally rational and non-ideally rational agents can have degrees of belief that are measured on something stronger than an ordinal scale, then we should also want an explanation that makes sense in both cases – a unifying theory is a better theory. There doesn't appear to be any difference in *meaning* when we say (e.g.) that Jules is *much more* confident in one proposition over another, depending on whether Jules is ideally rational or non-ideal like us. If that's right, then fundamentally the same explanation of quantitatability should apply in either case.

I intend for **Desideratum 4** to be compatible with the idea that there might be more than one adequate approach to the measurement of belief. It might be, for example, that a decision-theoretic approach is apt for the purposes of decision theory, and that an epistemic approach is apt for certain other theoretical contexts, with no fact of the matter as to which is the correct way of doing things. It's not unusual that there might be complementary ways of explaining the quantitation of a given quantity. For example, the ratio-scale measurement of mass can be explained as an instance of fundamental extensive measurement, or conjoint measurement, or (given an appropriate choice of base quantities) derived measurement – there is no fact of the matter as to which is the right way to do it. But the key term there is *complementary*. The various ways to explain the quantitation of mass are not disjunctive in the sense of giving one explanation for how mass is measured that applies to a certain subset of masses, and a fundamentally distinct explanation for other magnitudes. That's the kind of disjunctiveness we should avoid.

4 Epistemic Approaches: Comparative Confidence

The most straightforward and best-known of the epistemic approaches involves the probabilistic representation of (complete) binary comparative confidence relations. For ease of reference, I'll call this the *standard epistemic approach*. This section begins with an overview of the standard epistemic approach (Section 4.1), after which we consider the problem of logical omniscience and non-probabilistic generalisations (Section 4.2). Several further varieties of epistemic approach are discussed in the next section.

For the present section, we take $\succsim$ be interpreted relative to some agent α, and we read $p \succsim q$ as saying that α has at least as much confidence in p as she has in q. Supposing that $\succsim$ is a weak order, it's then natural to interpret $\succ$ as *more confidence*, and $\sim$ as *equal confidence*. Where $p \sim q$, I'll sometimes say that p and q are *equiprobable*; this shouldn't be understood to presuppose that $\succsim$ has a probabilistic representation.

4.1 Probabilistic Representations

The main results in this area concern the conditions under which a system comprised of an algebra of propositions and a comparative confidence relation, $\langle \mathcal{A}, \succsim \rangle$, can be represented in the numerical system $\langle \mathbb{R}^{\geq 0}, \geq \rangle$ by means of some probability measure. Savage (1954) established sufficient conditions, based on earlier work from de Finetti (1931). Kraft, Pratt, and Seidenberg (1959) were the first to provide necessary and sufficient conditions for the case of finite algebras, which were presented then in simpler form by Dana Scott (1964).

For the following definition, we take $\boldsymbol{p}^{\mathrm{i}}$ to be the *indicator function* of p. The indicator function of a proposition simply distinguishes those worlds that belong to the proposition from those that don't, by assigning 1 to the former and 0 to the latter; namely, $\boldsymbol{p}^{\mathrm{i}}$ is a function on Ω such that

$$\boldsymbol{p}^{\mathrm{i}}(\omega) = \begin{cases} 1 & \text{if } \omega \in p \\ 0 & \text{otherwise} \end{cases}.$$

Definition 9. Let $\mathcal{A}$ be an algebra of propositions on Ω, and $\succsim$ a binary relation on $\mathcal{A}$. Then $\langle \mathcal{A}, \succsim \rangle$ is a *finite system of qualitative probability* if and only if

1. $\mathcal{A}$ is finite   (*finitude*)
2. $\succsim$ is complete   (*completeness*)
3. $p \succsim \varnothing$ (*$\varnothing$-minimality*)
4. $\Omega > \varnothing$ (*non-triviality*)
5. If $p_1, \ldots, p_n$ and $q_1, \ldots, q_n$ are two sequences of propositions in $\mathcal{A}$, then, for $1 \leq j < n$, if

    i) $p_j \succsim q_j$, and
    ii) $\sum_{i=1}^{n} \boldsymbol{p}_i^{\mathrm{i}}(\omega) = \sum_{i=1}^{n} \boldsymbol{q}_i^{\mathrm{i}}(\omega)$ for all $\omega \in \Omega$,
    then $q_n \succsim p_n$ (*Scott's axiom*)

Theorem 10 (Scott 1964) $\langle \mathcal{A}, \succsim \rangle$ *is a finite system of qualitative probability if and only if at least one probability measure μ is a homomorphism from $\langle \mathcal{A}, \succsim \rangle$ into $\langle \mathbb{R}^{\geq 0}, \geq \rangle$.*

Much of the work is done by *Scott's axiom*, but what that axiom says isn't transparent. Roughly, it tells us that if two collections of propositions $p_1, \ldots, p_n$ and $q_1, \ldots, q_n$ contain the same number of truths as a matter of logical necessity, then if the agent is more confident of $n - 1$ propositions in the first collection than they are of the corresponding propositions in the second, there must be an nth proposition in the second collection of which they have more confidence than the corresponding proposition in the first collection – they must balance out. (Compare: for real values, if $x_1 + x_2 + x_3 = y_1 + y_2 + y_3$, and $x_1 \geq y_1$, $x_2 \geq y_2$, then $y_3 \geq x_3$.) But we needn't worry about what *Scott's axiom* says exactly; more illuminating for present purposes is to consider what the axiom implies in the context of the others.[14]

If we use $\sqcup$ henceforth to represent the union of disjoint sets – that is, the restriction of set-theoretic union $\cup$ to those pairs of sets with no elements in common – then for any finite system of qualitative probability,

1. $\succsim$ is a weak order   (*weak order*)
2. $p \sqcup (q \sqcup r) = (p \sqcup q) \sqcup r$ (*associativity*)
3. $p \sqcup q = q \sqcup p$ (*commutativity*)
4. $p \succsim q$ if and only if, if $r \cap (p \cup q) = \varnothing$ then $p \sqcup r \succsim q \sqcup r$ ($\sqcup$-*monotonicity*)
5. $p \sqcup q \succsim p$ (*weak positivity*)
6. $p \succsim p \sqcup q$ only if $q \sim \varnothing$ (*minimal identity*)

These should remind you of the properties that permit the additive measurement of length (Section 2.3), with $\sqcup$ playing something similar to role played by end-to-end concatenation in a positive concatenation structure. The *weak order* axiom is, as discussed earlier, necessary for $\succsim$ to be mapped into $\geq$. The *associativity* and *commutativity* axioms fall out of the associativity and commutativity of $\cup$. Finally, *weak positivity* and *minimal identity* correspond to the *non-negativity* condition in Definition 8 (the definition of a probability measure), while $\sqcup$-*monotonicity* corresponds to the $\sqcup$-*additivity* condition.

Indeed, we can make the analogy with the measurement of length more explicit by restating Theorem 10 thus:

Theorem 10′ $\langle \mathcal{A}, \succsim \rangle$ *is a finite system of qualitative probability if and only if there is at least one probability measure μ that is also a weak homomorphism from* $\langle \mathcal{A}, \succsim; \sqcup \rangle$ *into* $\langle \mathbb{R}^{\geq 0}, \geq; + \rangle$.

This way of stating Scott's result better captures the *point* of the probabilistic representation of comparative confidence. After all, if the goal was to show how a system $\langle \mathcal{A}, \succsim \rangle$ might be represented in $\langle \mathbb{R}^{\geq 0}, \geq \rangle$, then the *finitude* and *weak order* axioms would have sufficed – everything beyond that just serves to restrict the kinds of qualitative systems under consideration without making

---

[14] For extended exposition on *Scott's axiom*, see Titelbaum (2022, 491ff).

any difference to their *representability* in $\langle \mathbb{R}^{\geq 0}, \geq \rangle$. What makes it worthwhile to represent comparative confidence using a probability measure is that the characteristic properties of such measures (namely: $\sqcup$-*additivity*) are reflected in the 'additive' behaviour of $\succsim$ in relation to $\sqcup$, thus giving rise to meaning beyond just the ordering information. If not for this, then there's no apparent reason to care about probabilistic representations of $\succsim$ over any number of non-probabilistic but ordinally equivalent representations.

With that said, there's a couple important disanalogies with the case of length that should be noted. First, additive measures of $\langle \mathbf{L}, \succsim; \circ \rangle$ are *1-point unique* – that is, fixing the numerical value of any non-minimal length L will uniquely determine the remainder of the scale. The same needn't always be true for probabilistic measures of $\langle \mathcal{A}, \succsim; \sqcup \rangle$. Consider a finite algebra with atoms a_1, a_2, a_3, where

$$a_1 > (a_2 \cup a_3) > a_2 > a_3.$$

A probability measure μ will represent $\langle \mathcal{A}, \succsim; \sqcup \rangle$ just in case

$$1 > \mu(a_1) > \frac{1}{2} > \mu(a_2 \cup a_3) > \mu(a_2) > \mu(a_3) > 0.$$

Obviously, choosing a measure μ such that $\mu(a_1) = \frac{2}{3}$, for instance, won't yet determine the values for a_2 and a_3 – it only determines that they'll take distinct positive values summing to $\frac{1}{3}$. So the measure isn't 1-point unique. Essentially similar examples can be constructed to show that there will be systems of finite probability such that the additive measures of $\langle \mathcal{A}, \succsim; \sqcup \rangle$ are not *n*-point unique for arbitrarily large *n*.

Second, + is *meaningful* relative to the additive measures of $\langle \mathbf{L}, \succsim; \circ \rangle$, but the same needn't be true for probabilistic measures of $\langle \mathcal{A}, \succsim; \sqcup \rangle$. In other words, where μ and μ' are distinct probabilistic representations of the same system $\langle \mathcal{A}, \succsim; \sqcup \rangle$, the relation $R(+, \mu)$ induced on $\mathcal{A}$ by + relative to μ need not be the relation $R(+, \mu')$ induced on $\mathcal{A}$ by + relative to μ'. (Recall from Definition 6 that $(p, q, r) \in R(+, \mu)$ if and only if $\mu(p) + \mu(q) = \mu(r)$.) Consider again the previous example, where $\mu(a_1) = \frac{2}{3}$, and so

$$\mu(a_2 \cup a_3) + \mu(a_2 \cup a_3) = \mu(a_1).$$

Now suppose that μ' is such that $\mu'(a_1) = \frac{3}{4}$; hence

$$\mu'(a_2 \cup a_3) + \mu'(a_2 \cup a_3) \neq \mu'(a_1).$$

Though both μ and μ' are weakly additive measures of $\langle \mathcal{A}, \succsim; \sqcup \rangle$, the qualitative relation corresponding to + under μ isn't identical to the qualitative relation corresponding to + under μ'. So addition isn't $\langle \mathcal{A}, \succsim; \sqcup \rangle$-meaningful relative to $\langle \mathbb{R}^{\geq 0}, \geq; + \rangle$.

Both disanalogies are a result of the fact that probabilistic representations of a system of qualitative probability need not be unique. This situation can be remedied if we add more axioms, such as

- $p \gtrsim q$ only if $p \sim q \cup r$ for some $r \in \mathcal{A}$.   (*solvability*)

Supposing that $\langle \mathcal{A}, \gtrsim \rangle$ is a finite system of qualitative probability satisfying *solvability*, then the analogy with the additive measurement of length is considerably stronger. In that case, the set of weakly additive measures of $\langle \mathcal{A}, \gtrsim; \sqcup \rangle$ will include all and only those φ that are related to μ by a positive similarity transformation, and hence they will be 1-point unique (Suppes 1969, 6–7). Furthermore, $R(+, \mu) = R(+, \varphi)$ for any φ related to μ by a positive similarity transformation, and so + will be meaningful relative to any set of weakly additive measures of $\langle \mathcal{A}, \gtrsim; \sqcup \rangle$.

Another way to make that analogy clear is to generalise $\sqcup$ slightly, and then show that this generalised relation can be (strongly) mapped into +. Start with the following:

Definition 11. Where $\sim$ is an equivalence relation and $\bullet$ is a binary operation, $\bullet \backslash \sim$ is the *relation induced by* $\bullet$ *and* $\sim$ if and only if $(p, q, r) \in \bullet \backslash \sim$ whenever $p' \bullet q' \sim r$ for some p' and q' such that $p \sim p'$ and $q \sim q'$.

In the special case where $\sim$ is antisymmetric, there's no difference between $\bullet$ and $\bullet \backslash \sim$. For example, $+ \backslash =$ is just the same as +. But since the equiprobability of p and q need not imply the identity of p and q, in many cases it will be impossible to construct a system $\langle \mathcal{A}, \gtrsim; \bullet \rangle$ that admits of an additive measure in the stronger sense. For suppose $p \bullet q = r$, but there also exists some $s \neq r$ such that $r \sim s$. Then, if φ maps $\gtrsim$ into $\geq$, then $\bullet$ will strongly map into + only if $\varphi(p) + \varphi(q) = \varphi(s)$ implies $p \bullet q = s$, which by hypothesis is false. But this isn't a deep problem – we dissolve it entirely by mapping the very slightly more general ternary relation $\bullet \backslash \sim$ into + instead (where the latter is construed this time as a ternary relation). Thus,

Theorem 12 *Suppose that $\langle \mathcal{A}, \gtrsim \rangle$ is a finite system of qualitative probability satisfying* solvability. *Then there exists a homomorphism φ from $\langle \mathcal{A}, \gtrsim, \sqcup \backslash \sim \rangle$ into $\langle \mathbb{R}^{\geq 0}, \geq, + \rangle$. Furthermore, the set of all homomorphisms from $\langle \mathcal{A}, \gtrsim, \sqcup \backslash \sim \rangle$ into $\langle \mathbb{R}^{\geq 0}, \geq, + \rangle$ is unique up to positive similarity transformations, and exactly one of them is a probability measure.*

Proof. Suppose that μ is the unique probability representation of $\langle \mathcal{A}, \gtrsim \rangle$, guaranteed by the hypothesis of the theorem. The relation $R(+, \mu)$ always maps into

+ by definition, so for the existence result we need only establish $R(+,\mu) = \sqcup\backslash\sim$. To that end, note $(p,q,r) \in R(+,\mu)$ if and only if there exist $p',q',r \in \mathcal{A}$ such that $p' \sim p$, $q' \sim q$, $p' \cap q' = \varnothing$, and $p' \cup q' \sim r$. The right-to-left of that biconditional is trivial, given that $\geq$ represents $\succsim$ and that μ satisfies $\sqcup$-*additivity*. For the left-to-right, suppose $\mu(p) + \mu(q) = \mu(r)$. Where $p \cap q = \varnothing$, let $p = p'$, $q = q'$ and $r = p \cup q$. Where $p \cap q \neq \varnothing$, let s be a proposition such that $s \cap (p \cup q) = \varnothing$ and $s \sim p \cap q$. Using *solvability* it can be shown some such s exists. Now let $p' = p$, $q' = (q \cup s) - p$, and $r = p \cup q' = p \sqcup q'$. The proof of the uniqueness result is straightforward and omitted.   □

Note, though, that *solvability* isn't necessary for unique probabilistic representation. This is a good thing, since the axiom is very restrictive – in the context of the other axioms, it requires every atom of $\mathcal{A}$ that's non-minimal in $\succsim$ to be equiprobable with every other such atom. In other words, it forces all non-minimal atoms into a single $\sim$-equivalence class (Suppes 1969, 6–7). A more general condition that also suffices for unique probabilistic representability can be formulated in terms of *scalability*.

Definition 13. Suppose $r_1,\ldots,r_n$ is any sequence of pairwise disjoint and equiprobable propositions where $(r_1 \sqcup \ldots \sqcup r_n) \sim q$. Then,

1. If $p \sim r_i$, for $i = 1,\ldots,n$, then p is *directly scaled* by q
2. If p is directly scaled by q, then p is *scaled* by q
3. If p is scaled by q, and q is scaled by r, then p is scaled by r

In other words, the *scaling* relation is the ancestral of the *direct scaling* relation. The more general axiom can now be stated with ease:

- For any non-minimal atom $a \in \mathcal{A}$, a is scaled by Ω.   (*scalability*)

The difference between *solvability* and *scalability* is represented in Figure 4. We assume in each case that $\langle \mathcal{A}, \succsim \rangle$ is a finite system of qualitative probability, with the $\succsim$-ordering over the atoms of $\mathcal{A}$ represented by the relative size of the

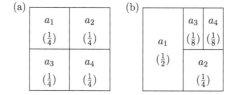

Figure 4 *Solvability* (a) versus *scalability* (b)

corresponding areas inside the box. On the left, case (a), *solvability* is satisfied, and hence also *scalability*. There are four equiprobable non-minimal atoms, a_1 to a_4, all directly scaled by Ω. Since $\mu(\Omega) = 1$, each atom must be assigned $\frac{1}{4}$ by any probability measure μ. Case (b) violates *solvability*, since

$$(a_1 \cup a_2 \cup a_3) \succsim (a_3 \cup a_4),$$

but there's no p such that

$$(a_1 \cup a_2 \cup a_3) \sim (a_3 \cup a_4 \cup p).$$

However, case (b) still satisfies *scalability*, and has a unique probabilistic representation. There are four atoms. The largest, a_1, is directly scaled by Ω, since a_1 and $(a_2 \cup a_3 \cup a_4)$ are disjoint, equiprobable, and their union is identical to and thus equiprobable with Ω. So $\mu(a_1) = \frac{1}{2}$. The second largest atom a_2 is then directly scaled by a_1:

$$\frac{1}{2} \cdot \frac{1}{2} = \frac{1}{4}.$$

Finally, a_3 and a_4 are both directly scaled by a_2 and thus assigned

$$\frac{1}{4} \cdot \frac{1}{2} = \frac{1}{8}.$$

As with *solvability*, *scalability* isn't necessary for unique probabilistic representability either. It turns out that necessary and sufficient conditions for unique probabilistic representations here are not easy to express (for reasons explained in Narens 1980), and we'll need to wait until we've introduced extended indicator functions in Section 5.2.

4.2 The Problem of Logical Omniscience

A probability measure on an algebra of sets $\mathcal{A}$ will always represent a comparative confidence ordering that extends the superset relation over the propositions in $\mathcal{A}$, in the sense that $p \supseteq q$ implies $p \succsim q$. Given **Assumption 1**, Ω includes only logically possible worlds. The combination of these facts presents a problem, since if Ω is restricted to possible worlds then $p \subseteq q$ if and only if p implies q. In other words, in the presence of **Assumption 1**, a probability measure can represent only logically omniscient agents – agents whose comparative confidence orderings invariably respect the logical relations between propositions.

Given the desiderata discussed in Section 3.4, it's therefore worth considering whether and how the standard epistemic approach might be generalised –

or better, *de-idealised* – so as to apply also to agents who aren't logically ideal. The generalisation I have in mind involves a tweak to how we understand the 'concatenation' operation. Basically, what we need to do is replace $\sqcup$ with a strictly more general operation that still allows for the same kind of additivity results that make the standard probabilistic approach interesting, while not also forcing logical omniscience.

Let me start by noting two important constraints. First, the concatenation operation ought to be *natural*. As explained in Section 2.4, without naturalness in the choice of qualitative primitives, the very idea of measurement is trivialised. Second, to avoid disjunctiveness (**Desideratum 4**), we are looking for a generalisation of the standard epistemic approach – specifically in the sense that we want a qualitative system $\langle \mathcal{A}, \succsim, R \rangle$ that can be represented in $\langle \mathbb{R}^{\geq 0}, \geq, + \rangle$, which includes qualitative probability structures as a special case, but which also allows for the non-probabilistic representation of structures that are not probabilistically representable. So we need a natural relation R that's an extension of $\sqcup$ in those cases (or at least some of those cases) where $\langle \mathcal{A}, \succsim; \sqcup \rangle$ does admit probabilistic representation.

These are not trivial constraints. It's not easy to find a natural relation that has the aforementioned properties, and which doesn't lead us right back in to the problem of logical omniscience. To appreciate the difficulty here, consider what happens when $R = \sqcup \backslash \sim$. In this case, R is guaranteed to be an extension of $\sqcup$, as desired. However, mapping $\sqcup \backslash \sim$ into $+$ leads inevitably to logical omniscience. Since p and $\varnothing$ are always disjoint, $p \sqcup \varnothing$ is always defined; moreover, $\varnothing$ will be the identity element with respect to $\sqcup$ (i.e., for all p, $p \sqcup \varnothing = p$). Consequently, if φ is any additive measure of $\langle \mathcal{A}, \succsim, \sqcup \backslash \sim \rangle$, then $p \sqcup \varnothing = p$ implies $\varphi(p) + \varphi(\varnothing) = \varphi(p)$ implies $\varphi(\varnothing) = 0$. In other words, the identity element of $\sqcup$ will need to be mapped to the identity element of $+$, which is zero. Furthermore, for any $p, q \in \mathcal{A}$, if $q \subseteq p$ then there will exist some $r \in \mathcal{A}$ such that $q \sqcup r = p$, hence $\varphi(q) + \varphi(r) = \varphi(p)$ and so $\varphi(p) \geq \varphi(q)$ and so $p \succsim q$. The result: $p \supseteq q$ implies $p \succsim q$; logical omniscience.

If we're to avoid logical omniscience, then $\sqcup$ cannot be what 'plays the concatenation role'. We do better if we consider instead the union of *subjectively incompatible* propositions. Henceforth, let $\uplus$ designate this operation, defined relative to $\succsim$ as the restriction of $\cup$ to those pairs of propositions p, q such that $p \cap q$ is minimal in $\succsim$. Intuitively, p and q are subjectively incompatible whenever the subject has at least as much confidence in any proposition whatsoever as they do in the conjunction of p and q. Then, $\uplus$ is an extension of $\sqcup$ whenever $\langle \mathcal{A}, \succsim; \sqcup \rangle$ can be represented probabilistically, as required. In other cases, though, $p \sqcup q = r$ needn't imply $p \uplus q = r$. Hence, it's possible to have an additive mapping from $\langle \mathcal{A}, \succsim, \uplus \backslash \sim \rangle$ into $\langle \mathbb{R}^{\geq 0}, \geq, + \rangle$ that needn't satisfy $\sqcup$-*additivity* in all cases, but which is also guaranteed to satisfy ⊔-*additivity* in those cases where a probabilistic representation of $\langle \mathcal{A}, \succsim, \uplus \setminus \sim \rangle$ exists.[15]

I'll start with a simple example, chosen to demonstrate that none of ∅-*minimality*, *non-triviality*, or *Scott's axiom* are required for the desired homomorphisms to exist. (As such, this is intended to be an extreme example, not a realistic one.) We suppose that $\mathcal{A}$ contains exactly four atoms, a_1 through a_4. We then label the non-atomic propositions via the indices of the atomic propositions from which they're constructed; so, for instance,

$$p_{\langle 234 \rangle} = a_2 \cup a_3 \cup a_4.$$

Given that, consider the following non-omniscient confidence ranking:

$$
\begin{bmatrix} \Omega \\ \varnothing \end{bmatrix} >
\begin{bmatrix} a_1 \\ a_2 \\ a_4 \\ p_{\langle 134 \rangle} \\ p_{\langle 234 \rangle} \end{bmatrix} >
\begin{bmatrix} p_{\langle 12 \rangle} \\ p_{\langle 14 \rangle} \\ p_{\langle 24 \rangle} \\ p_{\langle 34 \rangle} \\ p_{\langle 123 \rangle} \end{bmatrix} >
\begin{bmatrix} p_{\langle 13 \rangle} \\ p_{\langle 23 \rangle} \\ p_{\langle 124 \rangle} \end{bmatrix} > a_3.
$$

We want to show there's at least one $\varphi \colon \mathcal{A} \mapsto \mathbb{R}^{\geq 0}$ such that for all $p, q \in \mathcal{A}$,

    i. $p \succsim q$ if and only if $\varphi(p) \geq \varphi(q)$, and
    ii. $(p, q, r) \in \uplus \setminus \sim$ if and only if $\varphi(p) + \varphi(q) = \varphi(r)$.

It's clear the following assignment would satisfy property i:

$$\varphi(\Omega) = 1, \quad \varphi(a_1) = \frac{3}{4}, \quad \varphi(p_{\langle 12 \rangle}) = \frac{1}{2}, \quad \varphi(p_{\langle 13 \rangle}) = \frac{1}{4}, \quad \varphi(a_3) = 0.$$

So we just need to show that this assignment also satisfies property ii. To that end, note that p and q are subjectively incompatible only if they both include the minimal proposition a_3; for all the other propositions, it matters not where they sit in the $\succsim$ ordering (so long as they don't sit at the bottom). Hence, we need only consider the ordering of the *concatenable* propositions:

$$
\Omega >
\begin{bmatrix} p_{\langle 134 \rangle} \\ p_{\langle 234 \rangle} \end{bmatrix} >
\begin{bmatrix} p_{\langle 34 \rangle} \\ p_{\langle 123 \rangle} \end{bmatrix} >
\begin{bmatrix} p_{\langle 13 \rangle} \\ p_{\langle 23 \rangle} \end{bmatrix} > a_3.
$$

It's then easy to check that $\varphi(p \uplus q) = \varphi(p) + \varphi(q)$; and whenever $\varphi(p) + \varphi(q) = \varphi(r)$, then $(p, q, r) \in \uplus \setminus \sim$. Thus, it's possible to have a weakly additive (but not ⊔-*additive*) measure of $\langle \mathcal{A}, \succsim; \uplus \rangle$. More generally, it's possible to have a

---

[15] Every homomorphic mapping from $\langle \mathcal{A}, \succsim, \uplus \setminus \sim \rangle$ into $\langle \mathbb{R}^{\geq 0}, \geq, + \rangle$ is a *weakly* additive measure of $\langle \mathcal{A}, \succsim; \uplus \rangle$. For the reasons discussed earlier, strongly additive measures of $\langle \mathcal{A}, \succsim; \uplus \rangle$ will often be impossible inasmuch as $\succsim$ needn't be antisymmetric.

(strong) homomorphism from $\langle \mathcal{A}, \succsim, \uplus \backslash \sim \rangle$ into $\langle \mathbb{R}^{\geq 0}, \geq, + \rangle$, even while $\succsim$ is not logically omniscient.

The construction makes use of the same general notion of *scaling* from the previous section, though this time understood in terms of pairwise subjectively incompatible propositions rather than pairwise disjoint propositions. For example, $p_{\langle 34 \rangle}$ and $p_{\langle 123 \rangle}$ are equiprobable and subjectively incompatible, and their union is Ω; hence, they're directly scaled by Ω:

$$\varphi(p_{\langle 34 \rangle}) = \varphi(p_{\langle 123 \rangle}) = \frac{1}{2}\varphi(\Omega).$$

Then, $p_{\langle 13 \rangle}$ and $p_{\langle 23 \rangle}$ are equiprobable and subjectively incompatible, and their union is $p_{\langle 123 \rangle}$; hence, they're scaled by $p_{\langle 123 \rangle}$ and derivatively scaled by Ω:

$$\varphi(p_{\langle 13 \rangle}) = \varphi(p_{\langle 123 \rangle}) = \frac{1}{4}\varphi(\Omega).$$

The value for $p_{\langle 134 \rangle}$ can then be determined by summing the values for the subjectively incompatible propositions $p_{\langle 13 \rangle}$ and $p_{\langle 34 \rangle}$; that is,

$$\frac{1}{4}\varphi(\Omega) + \frac{1}{2}\varphi(\Omega) = \frac{3}{4}\varphi(\Omega).$$

Similar applies to $p_{\langle 234 \rangle}$. And, finally, the value for every other proposition is determined via equiprobability with some proposition whose value has already been fixed via scaling relative to Ω. So what makes the avoidance of logical omniscience possible here is that subjective incompatability needn't coincide with logical incompatibility. They *will* coincide whenever $\langle \mathcal{A}, \succsim; \sqcup \rangle$ can be represented probabilistically, but not always. Thus we can generalise the case of probabilistic representations by swapping out $\sqcup$ as the concatenation operation for the more general $\uplus$ operation.

Sufficient conditions for the existence of such representations are established in the following definition and associated theorem. There are three structural conditions – *finitude*, *richness*, and *weak solvability* – all of which are satisfied in the foregoing example.

Definition 14. Let $\mathcal{A}$ be an algebra of propositions on Ω, and $\succsim$ a binary relation on $\mathcal{A}$. Then $\langle \mathcal{A}, \succsim \rangle$ is a *finite system of additive confidence* if and only if $\mathcal{A}$ is finite and for all $p, q, r, s \in \mathcal{A}$,

1. $\succsim$ is a weak order   (*weak order*)
2. If $p \uplus q$ is defined, $p \succsim r$ and $q \succsim s$, then there are r' and s' such that $r' \uplus s'$ is defined, $r \sim r'$, and $s \sim s'$ (*richness*)
3. If $p > q$, then there are q' and r such that $q' \uplus r$ is defined, $q' \sim q$ and $p \succsim q' \sqcup r$ (*weak solvability*)

4. If $p \uplus r$ and $q \uplus r$ are defined and $p \gtrsim q$, then $p \cup r \gtrsim q \cup r$ ($\uplus$-*monotonicity*)

5. If $p \uplus q$ is defined, then $p \cup q \gtrsim p$, with $p \gtrsim p \cup q$ only if q is minimal

($\uplus$-*positivity*)

Theorem 15 *If $\langle \mathcal{A}, \gtrsim \rangle$ is a finite system of additive confidence, then there exists a homomorphism from $\langle \mathcal{A}, \gtrsim, \uplus \backslash \sim \rangle$ into $\langle \mathbb{R}^{\geq 0}, \geq, + \rangle$; furthermore, the set of all such homomorphisms is unique up to positive similarity transformations.*

Proof. The finer details of the proof are not especially illuminating, so I provide a summary. The strategy is to reconstruct $\langle \mathcal{A}, \gtrsim, \uplus \backslash \sim \rangle$ as a system for which strongly additive measures are known to exist. First we let $\mathbf{A} = \{\mathbf{p}, \mathbf{q}, \ldots\}$ be the set of $\sim$-equivalence classes in $\mathcal{A}$, with the minimal elements excised; that is, $\mathbf{p} = \{q \in \mathcal{A} \mid q \sim p\}$, with $\mathbf{p} \in \mathbf{A}$ only if $p > \varnothing$. We then let $\gtrsim$ be the total order induced on $\mathbf{A}$ by $\gtrsim$; that is, $\mathbf{p} \gtrsim \mathbf{q}$ whenever $p \gtrsim q$. C is to be interpreted as the set of concatenable pairs in $\mathbf{A}$, so $(\mathbf{p}, \mathbf{q}) \in C$ just when $p' \uplus q'$ is defined for some $p' \in \mathbf{p}$ and $q' \in \mathbf{q}$, or (same thing) when $(p, q, r) \in \uplus \backslash \sim$ for some r. Finally, $\circ$ is an operation on $\mathbf{A}$ such that $\mathbf{p} \circ \mathbf{q} = \mathbf{r}$ if and only if $(p, q, r) \in \uplus \backslash \sim$, and so a function from C into $\mathbf{A}$. We then want to show that $\langle \mathbf{A}, \gtrsim, C; \circ \rangle$ satisfies:

A. $\gtrsim$ is a total order.

B. If $(\mathbf{p}, \mathbf{q}) \in C$, $\mathbf{p} \gtrsim \mathbf{r}$, and $\mathbf{q} \gtrsim \mathbf{s}$, then $(\mathbf{r}, \mathbf{s}) \in C$.

C. If $(\mathbf{r}, \mathbf{p}) \in C$, then if $\mathbf{p} \gtrsim \mathbf{q}$, $\mathbf{r} \circ \mathbf{p} \gtrsim \mathbf{r} \circ \mathbf{q}$.

D. If $(\mathbf{p}, \mathbf{r}) \in C$, then if $\mathbf{p} \gtrsim \mathbf{q}$, $\mathbf{p} \circ \mathbf{r} \gtrsim \mathbf{q} \circ \mathbf{r}$.

E. $(\mathbf{p}, \mathbf{q}), (\mathbf{p} \circ \mathbf{q}, \mathbf{r}) \in C$ if and only if $(\mathbf{q}, \mathbf{r}), (\mathbf{p}, \mathbf{q} \circ \mathbf{r}) \in C$, and when both hold then $(\mathbf{p} \circ \mathbf{q}) \circ \mathbf{r} = \mathbf{p} \circ (\mathbf{q} \circ \mathbf{r})$

F. If $(\mathbf{p}, \mathbf{q}) \in C$, then $\mathbf{p} \circ \mathbf{q} > \mathbf{p}$.

G. If $\mathbf{p} > \mathbf{q}$, then there exists an $\mathbf{r} \in \mathbf{A}$ such that $(\mathbf{q}, \mathbf{r}) \in C$ and $\mathbf{p} \gtrsim \mathbf{q} \circ \mathbf{r}$.

Condition A follows from *weak order*, and B from *richness*. Given B, conditions C and D follow from $\uplus$-*monotonicity* and the commutativity of $\cap$ and $\cup$. The first conjunct of E falls out of how $\circ$ has been defined, and the second conjunct follows from the associativity of $\cap$ and $\cup$. Condition F is fixed by $\uplus$-*positivity*, and G by *weak solvability*. From these seven conditions plus *finitude*, it follows that the system $\langle \mathbf{A}, \gtrsim, C; \circ \rangle$ is a *Archimedean, regular, positive, ordered local semigroup* (Krantz *et al.* 1971, 44–5). This suffices for the existence of a homomorphism ψ from $\langle \mathbf{A}, \gtrsim; \circ \rangle$ into $\langle \mathbb{R}^{>0}, \geq; + \rangle$, and the set of such homomorphisms is unique up to positive similarity transformations. (This is a corollary of Krantz *et al.* 1971, 44–6, theorem 4 and theorem 4'.) We then let φ be defined on $\mathcal{A}$ such that $\varphi(p) = \psi(\mathbf{p})$ for all non-minimal p, and $\varphi(p) = 0$ otherwise, which gives us a homomorphism from $\langle \mathcal{A}, \gtrsim, \uplus \backslash \sim \rangle$ into $\langle \mathbb{R}^{\geq 0}, \geq, + \rangle$, and inherits the uniqueness properties mentioned earlier. $\square$

If $\langle \mathcal{A}, \gtrsim; \sqcup \rangle$ is a finite system of qualitative probability that also satisfies *solvability*, then it will be a finite system of additive confidence. In that case, the unique representation φ of $\langle \mathcal{A}, \gtrsim, \uplus \backslash \sim \rangle$ in $\langle \mathbb{R}^{\geq 0}, \geq, + \rangle$ that satisfies *normalisation* just is the unique probability representation of $\langle \mathcal{A}, \gtrsim; \sqcup \rangle$. From the perspective of the desiderata in Section 3.4, these are all good things.

However, it's not all happy news. While Theorem 15 offers a step forward in dealing with logical omniscience, it's no great leap. We've managed to avoid the strictest form of logical omniscience – that is, where $p \supseteq q$ always implies $p \gtrsim q$ – but the additive representation of $\langle \mathcal{A}, \gtrsim, \uplus \backslash \sim \rangle$ is perhaps not as flexible as one might like. For one thing, note that Ω will always be maximal in $\gtrsim$. To see why, suppose it isn't. A proposition p is *concatenable* just in case it's a superset of q for some q that's minimal in $\gtrsim$. The concatenable propositions are those that can stand in relations of subjective incompatibility, and in a finite system of additive confidence, every proposition must be equiprobable with a concatenable proposition. So, if Ω isn't maximal in $\gtrsim$, then at least one other concatenable proposition must be. Let p_{max} be that proposition, or one of them, and let p_{min} be any minimal proposition that implies p_{max}. Now suppose q is $(\Omega \backslash p_{max}) \cup p_{min}$. So q and p_{max} are subjectively incompatible, and we should have $\varphi(p) + \varphi(q) = \varphi(p \cup q)$; but $p \cup q = \Omega$, so $\varphi(\Omega) \geq \varphi(p)$, contradicting the hypothesis that $p_{max} > \Omega$.

More generally, in any finite system of additive confidence, $q \subseteq p$ will always entail $p \gtrsim q$ *with respect to* pairs of concatenable propositions p and q. So while we've shown that it's possible to maintain the analogy with the measurement of length while avoiding logical omniscience, the results here are still quite limited. What we really have in the end is not non-omniscience but a restricted form of omniscience. Moreover, this means that any time $\varnothing$ is minimal, then the stricter form of logical omniscience follows immediately – since in that case *every* proposition in the algebra is automatically concatenable.

Other generalisations of the standard epistemic approach *might* be possible, though the relevant work has yet to be done. The difficulty, as I said, is locating an appropriately natural operation to 'play the concatenation role', which generalises the probabilistic case but doesn't force logical omniscience (or something near as bad). Not an easy thing to find, when the most natural operations in the vicinity seem to be set-theoretic relations between contents that, given **Assumption 1**, correspond directly to their logical relationships. Maybe that's a good reason to revisit **Assumption 1**. But if it is, then it's also a good reason to consider alternative measurement structures that don't rely so much on set-theoretic relations between belief contents.

5 Epistemic Approaches: Alternatives

Epistemic approaches to the measurement of belief aren't limited to those involving a single binary confidence relation. In this section, I briefly look at several other epistemic approaches. The first involves quarternary (or conditional) confidence relations (Section 5.2); then qualitative expectation relations (Section 5.1); then structures involving multiple primitive doxastic relations (Section 5.3).

5.1 Conditional Confidence

A theory of belief measurement that makes use of a binary confidence relation will be well-suited for representations that assign a single numerical value to each proposition, where this is intended to represent the agent's *unconditional* confidence regarding that proposition. However, it's sometimes thought that the more fundamental concept in epistemology is not unconditional confidence but rather conditional confidence – the level of confidence one has in *p given* some hypothesis q (e.g., Hájek 2003). A common motivation for this thought is that, while it's standard to define conditional probabilities out of unconditional probabilities like so,

$$\mu(p|q) = \frac{\mu(p \cap q)}{\mu(q)},$$

that definition only makes sense when $\mu(q) > 0$; yet there appear to be cases where it makes sense to speak of the probability of p conditional on q even while the unconditional probability of q is zero.

There is an epistemic approach to the measurement of belief that fits nicely with this perspective. It involves replacing the binary confidence relation of the standard epistemic approach with a quarternary relation – or, same thing, a binary relation $\succsim$ on $\mathcal{A} \times \mathcal{A}$, interpreted

$(p, q) \succsim (r, s)$ if and only if α is at least as confident in p given q as she is in r given s.

To make things a little easier, let's write $p|q \succsim r|s$ instead. The goal, then, is to lay down axioms on this quarternary $\succsim$ that will suffice for the 'probabilistic' representation thereof. Much of the work done on this matter is owing to Koopman – see especially his (1940a) and (1940b); see also (Luce 1968). For this section, however, I will briefly summarise a more recent (but closely related) result in Hawthorne (2016).[16]

---

[16] Hawthorne interprets $\succsim$ as a relation of comparative evidential support between premises and conclusions. As he notes, though, the formalism can be interpreted in many ways.

Since we are treating conditional probabilities as basic, the numerical representation cannot consist in probability measures strictly so-called (i.e., as per Definition 8). Instead, we employ *Popper functions*, which generalise the classic definition of a probability measure:

Definition 16. $\pi\colon \mathcal{A}\times\mathcal{A} \mapsto \mathbb{R}$ is a *Popper function* if and only if

1. For some $p,q,r,s \in \mathcal{A}$, $\pi(p|q) \neq \pi(r|s)$
2. For all $p,q,r \in \mathcal{A}$, $\pi(p|p) \geq \pi(q|r)$
3. If $q \subseteq p$, then $\pi(p|r) \geq \pi(q|r)$
4. $\pi(p|q) + \pi(\neg p|q) = \pi(q|q)$ unless $\pi(r|q) = \pi(q|q)$ for all $r \in \mathcal{A}$
5. $\pi(p \cap q|r) = \pi(p|q \cap r) \times \pi(q|r)$

Relative to a fixed condition, a Popper function behaves essentially like a probability measure. For instance, fixing the condition to Ω, the definition implies:

- $\pi(p|\Omega) \in [0,1]$,
- $\pi(\Omega|\Omega) = 1$, and
- if $p \cap q = \varnothing$, then $\pi(p \cup q|\Omega) = \pi(p|\Omega) + \pi(q|\Omega)$.

Moreover, if μ is the probability measure corresponding to $\pi(\cdot|\Omega)$, then for any p such that $\pi(p|\Omega) > 0$, $\pi(q|p)$ will behave just like $\mu(q|p)$. The difference, though, is that $\pi(q|p)$ can still be defined even when $\pi(p|\Omega) = 0$. In this case, $\pi(\cdot|p)$ *also* behaves just like a probability measure μ', different from μ, in the same way that $\pi(\cdot|\Omega)$ behaves like μ. And likewise, there may be some r such that $\pi(r|p) = 0$, and $\pi(\cdot|r)$ might behave in turn like yet another probability measure different again from μ' and μ. Thus the Popper function π can act like an ordered hierarchy of probability measures. As Hawthorne helpfully puts it,

> a Popper function may consist of a ranked hierarchy of classical probability functions, where conditionalization on a probability 0 sentence induces a transition from one classical probability function to another classical function at a lower rank. The idea is that probability 0 need not mean 'absolutely impossible'. Rather, it means something like, 'not a viable possibility unless (and until) the more plausible alternatives are refuted.' (2016, 281)

See also van Fraassen (1976), Spohn (1986), Halpern (2001), and Brickhill and Horsten (2018) for detailed discussion on the close relationship between Popper functions, lexicographic probability measures (lexically ordered sequences of

---

See DiBella (2018) for a quarternary $\succsim$ explicitly interpreted as comparative conditional confidence.

probabilities), and non-Archimedean probability measures (probabilities that can take infinitesimal numerical values).

As one might naturally expect, the additional complexity of the numerical representation – with Definition 16 including both an additive component in condition 4, and a multiplicative component in condition 5 – corresponds to significant increased complexity in the required axioms on $\succsim$:

Definition 17. Let $\mathcal{A}$ be an algebra of propositions on Ω, and $\succsim$ a binary relation on $\mathcal{A} \times \mathcal{A}$. We say that $\langle \mathcal{A} \times \mathcal{A}, \succsim \rangle$ is a *system of qualitative conditional probability* if and only if the following are satisfied:

1. $\succsim$ is a weak order $\hfill$ (*weak order*)
2. For some $p, q, r, s \in \mathcal{A}$, $p|q > r|s$ $\hfill$ (*non-triviality*)
3. For all $p, q \in \mathcal{A}$, $p|p \succsim q|p$ $\hfill$ (*maximality*)
4. For all $p, q, r \in \mathcal{A}$, if $p \subseteq q$, then $q|r \succsim p|r$ $\hfill$ (*implication*)
5. For all $p, q, r, s \in \mathcal{A}$, if $p|q \succsim r|s$ and $q \neq \varnothing$, then $\neg r|s \succsim \neg p|q$

$\hfill$ (*negation-symmetry*)

6. For all $p_1, q_1, r_1, p_2, q_2, r_2 \in \mathcal{A}$, if

    i) $p_1|(q_1 \cap r_1) \succsim p_2|(q_2 \cap r_2)$ and $q_1|r_1 \succsim q_2|r_2$, or

    ii) $p_1|(q_1 \cap r_1) \succsim q_2|r_2$ and $q_1|r_1 \succsim p_2|(q_2 \cap r_2)$,

  then $(p_1 \cap q_1)|r_1 \succsim (p_2 \cap q_2)|r_2$ $\hfill$ (*composition*)

7. For all $p_1, q_1, r_1, p_2, q_2, r_2 \in \mathcal{A}$, if $(p_1 \cap q_1)|r_1 \succsim (p_2 \cap q_2)|r_2$ and $r_2 \not\subseteq \neg q_2$, and

    i) if $q_2|r_2 \succsim q_1|r_1$, then $p_1|(q_1 \cap r_1) \succsim p_2|(q_2 \cap r_2)$

    ii) if $q_2|r_2 \succsim p_1|(q_1 \cap r_1)$, then $q_1|r_1 \succsim p_2|(q_2 \cap r_2)$ (*decomposition-a*)

8. For all $p_1, q_1, r_1, p_2, q_2, r_2 \in \mathcal{A}$, if $(p_1 \cap q_1)|r_1 \succsim (p_2 \cap q_2)|r_2$ and $(q_2 \cap r_2) \not\subseteq \neg p_2$, then

    i) if $p_2|(q_2 \cap r_2) \succsim p_1|(q_1 \cap r_1)$, then $q_1|r_1 \succsim q_2|r_2$

    ii) if $p_2|(q_2 \cap r_2) \succsim q_1|r_1$, then $p_1|(q_1 \cap r_1) \succsim q_2|r_2$ (*decomposition-b*)

9. For all $p, q, r, s \in \mathcal{A}$, if $p|q > r|s$, then for some $n \geq 2$ there exist $t_1, \ldots, t_n$, $u \in \mathcal{A}$ such that

    i) $u|u > \neg t_1|u$,

    ii) for distinct $i, j = 1, \ldots, n$, $t_i|u \sim t_j|u$ and $\neg(t_i \cap t_j)|u \succsim u|u$,

    iii) $(t_1 \cup \ldots \cup t_n)|u \succsim u|u$,

    iv) for some $m \leq n$, $p|q > (t_1 \cup \ldots \cup t_m)|u > r|s$ $\hfill$ (*Archimedean*)

Theorem 18 Hawthorne (2016) *If $\langle \mathcal{A} \times \mathcal{A}, \succsim \rangle$ is a system of qualitative conditional probability, there exists a homomorphism from $\langle \mathcal{A} \times \mathcal{A}, \succsim \rangle$ into $\langle \mathbb{R}^{\geq 0}, \geq \rangle$, and exactly one such homomorphism is a Popper function.*

The *non-triviality*, *maximality*, and *implication* axioms directly correspond to conditions 1, 2, and 3 of Definition 16. The *negation-symmetry* axiom is the main axiom corresponding to the additivity condition 4, while the *composition* and *decomposition* axioms correspond to the multiplicative condition. The *Archimedean* axiom says that whenever $p|q > r|s$, there is a finite number of mutually exclusive and equiprobable propositions such that the conditional probability of their union (relative to some condition) is strictly between that of $p|q$ and $r|s$. In terms of the representation: if $p|q > r|s$, then the difference between $\pi(p|q)$ and $\pi(r|s)$ is not infinitesimal, ensuring $\gtrsim$ can be represented in $\mathbb{R}$.

5.2 Qualitative Expectations

A rather different epistemic approach – originating with Suppes and Zanotti (1976), see also Clark (2000) and Suppes and Pederson (2016) – takes the primitive ordering relation $\gtrsim$ to be defined not over an algebra of propositions, but instead over an algebra of *extended indicator functions*.

Extended indicator functions are a generalisation of indicator functions. In the broadest terms, an extended indicator function is a certain kind of random variable – an integer-valued function f defined on Ω such that for some positive integer n, propositions $p_1, \ldots, p_n$, and non-negative integers $k_1, \ldots, k_n$,

$$f(\omega) = \sum_{j=1}^{n} k_j \cdot \boldsymbol{p}_j^{\mathrm{i}}(\omega).$$

But that's unlikely to be intuitive, so it'll help to consider how extended indicator functions can be built up via the pointwise summation of ordinary indicator functions. Start with the indicator function of p, or $\boldsymbol{p}^{\mathrm{i}}$, which in Section 4 was defined as the function that takes each world ω in Ω and returns the value 1 if ω belongs to p, and 0 otherwise. Now consider its nth iteration, $n\boldsymbol{p}^{\mathrm{i}}$, defined:

$$n\boldsymbol{p}^{\mathrm{i}}(\omega) = \overbrace{\boldsymbol{p}^{\mathrm{i}}(\omega) + \cdots + \boldsymbol{p}^{\mathrm{i}}(\omega)}^{n \text{ times}} = \begin{cases} n & \text{if } \omega \in p \\ 0 & \text{otherwise} \end{cases}$$

For any integer $n \geq 1$, the nth iteration of any indicator function will count as an extended indicator function. Clearly, where $n = 1$, then $1\boldsymbol{p}^{\mathrm{i}} = \boldsymbol{p}^{\mathrm{i}}$; and where $n > 1$, then $n\boldsymbol{p}^{\mathrm{i}}$ can be expressed as the pointwise sum of $m\boldsymbol{p}^{\mathrm{i}}$ and $k\boldsymbol{p}^{\mathrm{i}}$ (or $m\boldsymbol{p}^{\mathrm{i}} + k\boldsymbol{p}^{\mathrm{i}}$) for $m + k = n$. More generally, the pointwise sum of *any* two extended indicator functions will also count as an extended indicator function. So, for example, $n\boldsymbol{p}^{\mathrm{i}} + m\boldsymbol{q}^{\mathrm{i}}$ is an extended indicator function:

$$np^i(\omega) \dotplus mq^i(\omega) = np^i(\omega) + mq^i(\omega) = \begin{cases} n + m & \text{if } \omega \in p \text{ and } \omega \in q \\ n & \text{if } \omega \in p \text{ and } \omega \notin q \\ m & \text{if } \omega \notin p \text{ and } \omega \in q \\ 0 & \text{otherwise} \end{cases}$$

In the same fashion, $(np^i \dotplus mq^i) \dotplus kr^i$ is an extended indicator function, and so on. Hence we can construct a space of extended indicator functions by starting with a set of propositions, taking the set of indicator functions corresponding to those propositions, and closing it under pointwise summation:

Definition 19. $\mathcal{A}^i$ is the *algebra of extended indicator functions generated by* $\mathcal{A}$ iff

1. For all $p \in \mathcal{A}$, $p^i \in \mathcal{A}^i$
2. If $f, g \in \mathcal{A}^i$, then $f \dotplus g \in \mathcal{A}^i$
3. Nothing else is in $\mathcal{A}^i$

This algebra of extended indicator functions will comprise the domain of the primitive binary relation $\succsim$ – a so-called *qualitative expectations* relation – with the goal being to represent $\succsim$ via an *expectation function*:

Definition 20. Where $\mathcal{A}^i$ is the algebra of extended indicator functions generated by $\mathcal{A}$, a function $\epsilon \colon \mathcal{A}^i \mapsto \mathbb{R}^{\geq 0}$ is an *expectation function* if and only if for all $x, y \in \mathcal{A}^i$,

1. $\epsilon(\Omega^i) > \epsilon(\varnothing^i) = 0$
2. $\epsilon(x \dotplus y) = \epsilon(x) + \epsilon(y)$

So we're mapping $\dotplus$ into $+$, in other words. Sufficient conditions for the existence of such representations are provided by the following theorem. Given the additive structure of the representation, these axioms should come as no surprise:

Definition 21. Let $\mathcal{A}$ be an algebra of propositions on Ω, and $\succsim$ a binary relation on the algebra $\mathcal{A}^i$ of extended indicator functions generated by $\mathcal{A}$. Then $\langle \mathcal{A}^i, \succsim \rangle$ is a *system of qualitative expectations* if and only if it satisfies the following, for all $x, y, z \in \mathcal{A}^i$,

1. $\succsim$ is a weak order   *(weak order)*
2. $x \succsim \varnothing^i$ *($\varnothing^i$-minimality)*

3. $\Omega^i > \varnothing^i$ *(non-triviality)*

4. $x \gtrsim y$ if and only if $x \dotplus z \gtrsim y \dotplus z$ *(+-monotonicity)*

5. If $x > y$, then there are $k, n \geq 1$ with $nx > k\Omega^i > ny$ *(Archimedean)*

Theorem 22 Suppes (2016) *If $\langle \mathcal{A}^i, \gtrsim \rangle$ is a system of qualitative expectations, then there is an expectation function that maps $\langle \mathcal{A}^i, \gtrsim \rangle$ into $\langle \mathbb{R}^{\geq 0}, \geq \rangle$; furthermore, the set of homomorphisms from $\langle \mathcal{A}^i, \gtrsim \rangle$ into $\langle \mathbb{R}^{\geq 0}, \geq \rangle$ that are also expectation functions is unique up to positive similarity transformations.*

Note that any expectation function which maps $\langle \mathcal{A}^i, \gtrsim \rangle$ into $\langle \mathbb{R}^{\geq 0}, \geq \rangle$ is ipso facto a weakly additive representation of $\langle \mathcal{A}^i, \gtrsim; \dotplus \rangle$ in $\langle \mathbb{R}^{\geq 0}, \geq; + \rangle$, and vice versa. Indeed, similar to the reformulation Theorem 10 as Theorem 10′ earlier, it would be straightforward to re-write Theorem 22 so as to make the connection with extensive measurement more transparent. Essentially: if $\langle \mathcal{A}^i, \gtrsim; \dotplus \rangle$ satisfies the stated axioms, then there is a weak homomorphism, unique up to a positive similarity transformation, from $\langle \mathcal{A}^i, \gtrsim; \dotplus \rangle$ into $\langle \mathbb{R}^{\geq 0}, \geq; + \rangle$.

There is a direct connection between expectation representations of qualitative expectation relations and the probabilistic representation of comparative confidence relations. Note that any expectation function ϵ is related by a positive similarity transformation to exactly one normalised expectation function ϵ', with $\epsilon'(\Omega^i) = 1$. This ϵ' describes a probability measure μ if, for all $p \in \mathcal{A}$, we let $\mu(p) = \epsilon'(\mathbf{p}^i)$. In other words, the weakly additive measures of $\langle \mathcal{A}^i, \gtrsim; \dotplus \rangle$ correspond to a unique probability measure on $\mathcal{A}$. Indeed, Suppes and Zanotti (1976, 435–7) were able to establish that $\langle \mathcal{A}, \gtrsim \rangle$ has a *unique* probabilistic representation if and only if there exists a system of qualitative expectations $\langle \mathcal{A}^i, \gtrsim \rangle$ such that $\gtrsim$ on $\mathcal{A}$ is the weak order induced by $\gtrsim$ on $\mathcal{A}^i$, defined like so:

$$p \gtrsim q \text{ iff } \mathbf{p}^i \gtrsim \mathbf{q}^i$$

So, a (complete) binary confidence relation is uniquely probabilistically representable just when it can be extended to a qualitative expectations relation which satisfies Suppes and Zanotti's five axioms.

So much for the formalities, now for the hard part: the interpretation of $\gtrsim$ over $\mathcal{A}^i$ isn't entirely transparent, and I suspect this is main reason why there's been comparatively little work done on this approach. In the usual case, random variables are functions from the outcomes of an experiment-type to numerical values of those outcomes. For instance, if we say the experiment is tossing two six-sided die, there are 36 possible outcomes corresponding to the different combinations, and 11 possible numerical values from 2 to 12 they might sum to. Letting $\mathbf{r}$ be the corresponding random variable, the expected value ϵ of $\mathbf{r}$ is the probability-weighted average value of the outcomes (under the supposition the experiment is run), and the sum of the expected value of r with itself n times can be interpreted as the expected total value of n independent runs of the same experiment under the same conditions. If the die are fair, then $\epsilon(r) = 7$, and

$$\epsilon(r \overline{+} r) = \epsilon(r) + \epsilon(r) = 14.$$

For this to make sense, though, it should be possible for those 36 outcomes to recur across independent instances of the same experiment. It is much less clear how to make sense of the iterated variables where the 'outcomes' are maximally specific possible worlds and the 'experiment', as such, can only be run once. Suppose p is the proposition *there are dogs*, and q the proposition *most roses are red*. Presumably we should be able to find both propositions in $\mathcal{A}$, given the intended interpretation of that set. Each corresponds to a random variable over Ω, namely p^i and q^i, and there's no difficulty in interpreting $p^i \gtrsim q^i$ as an expectation relation *in this case*. But the interpretations of $3p^i$ and $5q^i$ are not similarly transparent, and still less the interpretation of $3p^i \overline{+} 5q^i$.

In connection to this, it's noteworthy that Suppes (2014, 53) later flagged interpretive difficulties as a distinctive cost for the approach, particularly vis-à-vis the mixed indicator functions $p_j^i + q_j^i$. Suppes and Zanotti (1982) explain one possible way to interpret their mixed non-iterated functions $p^i \overline{+} q^i$ thus:

> Suppose Smith is considering two locations to fly to for a weekend vacation. Let p_j be the event of sunny weather at location j and q_j be the event of warm weather at location j. The qualitative comparison Smith is interested in is the expected value of $p_1^i + q_1^i$ *versus* the expected value of $p_2^i + q_2^i$. It's natural to insist that the utility of the outcomes has been too simplified by the sums $p_j^i + q_j^i$. The proper response is that the expected values of the two functions are being compared as a matter of belief, not value or utility. Thus it would seem quite natural to bet that the expected value of $p_1^i + q_1^i$ will be greater than that of $p_2^i + q_2^i$, no matter how one feels about the relative desirability of sunny versus warm weather. (p. 433)

And in regards to the non-mixed iterated indicator functions, np^i where $n > 1$, Suppes (2014) offers the following interpretation:

> From an intuitive estimation or gambling standpoint, it's much easier to reflect on the subjective probability of np^i than of $np^i \overline{+} mq^i$. For example, if $p^i(\omega) = 1$ means 'heads' in a toss of a coin with unknown bias, then $5p^i$ is just the estimate of 5 such tosses being 'heads'. (p. 53)

The 'heads' example is selectively chosen. Supposing Ω is a set of possible worlds, $p^i(\omega) = 1$ *in general* means that the proposition p is true at the world

ω. It is not clear to me how something along the lines of Suppes' suggested reading will make intuitive sense when p is *there are dogs* or *most roses are red*.

5.3 Multiprimitive Structures

Suppose we identify an agent's unconditional probabilities with their probabilities conditional on the necessary proposition Ω. Given that, we can usefully see the two epistemic accounts just discussed as alternative ways of enriching the relatively simple systems of unconditional comparative confidence $\langle \mathcal{A}, \succsim \rangle$ that were characterised by Definition 9. The account in Section 5.1 extends the domain of the confidence relation to $\mathcal{A} \times \mathcal{A}$, such that the agent's unconditional confidence ordering falls out as a special case. The qualitative expectations account in Section 5.2 instead extends the domain from $\mathcal{A}$ to $\mathcal{A}^i$, again with the unconditional confidence ordering being a special part of the richer relation. The following alternative also enriches the simple $\langle \mathcal{A}, \succsim \rangle$ systems, though in a different way again: by adding more psychological primitives to the system.

Of course, there is an absurd variety of ways this might go, depending on what primitives we choose to add and the structures we take them to have. One might conceivably add a primitive unary property corresponding to *certainty*, for example. Definitions of 'certainty' in terms of comparative confidence will usually equate it with maximal confidence, but one might imagine that *being certain that p* can sometimes come apart from *being at least as confident that p as any other proposition* – and so an independent primitive for qualitative certainty would be useful. Similarly, if one supposes that all-or-nothing belief is related but not reducible to comparative confidence, and therefore seeks to represent all-or-nothing beliefs alongside degrees of belief within a single numerical framework, then one might try adding a primitive *all-or-nothing believes* relation by which to do so. There's all sorts of things one might conceivably do.

Probably the most commonly suggested additional primitive, however, is an *independence* relation (e.g., Domotor 1970; Fine 1973; Kaplan & Fine 1977; Luce 1978; Luce & Narens 1978; Joyce 2010). Per usual, we say p and q are independent relative to a probability measure μ whenever

$$\mu(p \cap q) = \mu(p) \cdot \mu(q).$$

In cases where a comparative confidence relation can be represented by more than one probability measure, which propositions will count as probabilistically independent of one another can sometimes vary depending on which measures are chosen. An example: suppose $\mathcal{A}$ contains four atoms, a_1–a_4, and the probability measures μ and μ' are defined like so:

$$\mu(a_1) = 0.02, \quad \mu(a_2) = 0.08, \quad \mu(a_3) = 0.18, \quad \mu(a_4) = 0.72$$
$$\mu'(a_1) = 0.03, \quad \mu'(a_2) = 0.08, \quad \mu'(a_3) = 0.18, \quad \mu'(a_4) = 0.71$$

The resulting measures correspond to the same overall confidence ordering, as represented in the following table:

	μ	μ'		μ	μ'
Ω	1	1	$p_{\langle 123 \rangle}$	0.28	0.29
$p_{\langle 234 \rangle}$	0.98	0.97	$p_{\langle 23 \rangle}$	0.26	0.26
$p_{\langle 134 \rangle}$	0.92	0.92	$p_{\langle 13 \rangle}$	0.20	0.21
$p_{\langle 34 \rangle}$	0.90	0.89	a_3	0.18	0.18
$p_{\langle 124 \rangle}$	0.82	0.82	$p_{\langle 12 \rangle}$	0.10	0.11
$p_{\langle 24 \rangle}$	0.80	0.79	a_2	0.08	0.08
$p_{\langle 14 \rangle}$	0.74	0.74	a_1	0.02	0.03
a_4	0.72	0.71	$\varnothing$	0	0

Observe that $p_{\langle 24 \rangle}$ and $p_{\langle 34 \rangle}$ are independent relative to μ, not relative to μ':

$$\mu(a_4) = \mu(p_{\langle 24 \rangle}) \cdot \mu(p_{\langle 34 \rangle}), \quad \mu'(a_4) \neq \mu'(p_{\langle 24 \rangle}) \cdot \mu'(p_{\langle 34 \rangle})$$

So probabilistic independence is not, in general, *meaningful* relative to the probabilistic measurement of comparative confidence.

Since independence is one of the more central concepts in probability theory, and does important theoretical work, we should want to rectify this situation. One might suppose we can simply solve the problem by imposing further axioms on $\succsim$, thus ensuring a unique probabilistic representation. But this response is inadequate. For one thing, it doesn't solve the problem. Even supposing that $\langle \mathcal{A}, \succsim; \sqcup \rangle$ has a unique *probabilistic* representation in $\langle \mathbb{R}, \geq; + \rangle$, there will still be many non-probabilistic representations of that system in $\langle \mathbb{R}, \geq; + \rangle$ whereby $\varphi(\Omega)$ needn't equal 1 – so independence will not be meaningful relative to the natural class of additive homomorphisms into $\langle \mathbb{R}, \geq; + \rangle$.[17] Moreover, there will still be ordinally equivalent probability measures that

---

[17] See Luce *et al.* (1990, 277–8) for useful discussion on this point. As they note, one shouldn't infer meaningfulness from an arbitrary restriction on the additive homomorphisms (e.g., to the special case where $\varphi(\Omega) = 1$). If that sort of thing were admissible, we could quickly trivialise the notion of meaningfulness for any measure that's 1-point unique.

plausibly represent distinct systems of belief – as evidenced by their differentiable roles in epistemology and decision theory – and we should like to be able to account for them too.

The better response is to find a system of primitives that will guarantee meaningfulness for independence. Most obviously, we can include a primitive qualitative independence relation alongside comparative confidence. Let $\perp$ designate a binary relation on $\mathcal{A}$. The goal is then to supply conditions on an enriched system $\langle \mathcal{A}, \succsim, \perp \rangle$ sufficient for the existence of a measure φ such that

    i. $p \succsim q$ if and only if $\varphi(p) \geq \varphi(q)$
    ii. If $p \cap q = \varnothing$, then $\varphi(p \cup q) = \varphi(p) + \varphi(q)$
    iii. $p \perp q$ if and only if $\varphi(p \cap q) = \varphi(p) \cdot \varphi(q)$

If $\mathcal{A}$ is finite, then such a measure will exist only if $\succsim$ satisfies the axioms from Definition 9. Necessary axioms for $\perp$ on this interpretation are provided by Suppes (2014); each directly corresponds to basic properties of probabilistic independence:

1. $p \perp \Omega$
2. If $p \perp p$, then $p \sim \Omega$ or $p \sim \varnothing$
3. If $p \perp q$, then $q \perp p$
4. If $p \perp q$, then $p \perp \neg q$
5. If $q \cap r = \varnothing$, and $p \perp q, p \perp r$, then $p \perp q \cup r$

Including a primitive independence relation with these constraints into a system of qualitative probability will *in some cases* be enough to let us meaningfully differentiate between ordinally equivalent probability measures. It does for the preceding example, for instance, depending on whether $p_{\langle 12 \rangle} \perp p_{\langle 23 \rangle}$ or not. But it's not always enough. Consider again the case that was earlier discussed in Section 3.4, where $\mathcal{A} = \{\Omega, p, \neg p, \varnothing\}$ and

$$\Omega > p > \neg p > \varnothing.$$

Suppose that the $\mathcal{A}$ and $\succsim$ in $\langle \mathcal{A}, \succsim, \perp \rangle$ have this structure. Then $\langle \mathcal{A}, \succsim, \perp \rangle$ can be represented by numerous measures satisfying properties i and ii, provided

$$\varphi(\Omega) > \varphi(p) = \big(\varphi(\Omega) - \varphi(\neg p)\big) > \varphi(\varnothing) = 0.$$

The addition of property iii forces those measures to satisfy *normalisation*, and hence forces them all to be probability measures. However, it does nothing to sort between the many ordinally equivalent probability measures that fit with those comparative confidences.

It is possible to add yet further primitives that will help to guarantee unique probabilistic representability even where the conditions on $\succsim$ and $\perp$ alone are not enough. Suppes (2014, 49–50) shows that if one adds a primitive *entropic uncertainty* relation $\succsim^u$ (defined over partitions of Ω) alongside appropriate axioms relating $\succsim$, $\perp$, and $\succsim^u$, then one can guarantee a unique (absolute scale) representation of the resulting system that also happens to be a probability measure. No doubt there are many other primitives that one could try including alongside $\succsim$ and $\perp$ that might work too. The matter has so far only undergone the most cursory exploration.

6 Decision-Theoretic Approaches

A *decision-theoretic representation* is a kind of conjoint representation, typically of a single binary preference relation that decomposes into a representation of beliefs and a representation of (basic) desires that pairwise determine those preferences according to a pre-specified decision rule.

Decision-theoretic representations can differ along several dimensions, depending on the primitives used to construct the qualitative system, the desired constraints on the numerical representations of belief and desire, or the details of the decision rule. By far the most well-known theorems in this space are those for subjective expected utility theory; here we find the seminal works of Ramsey (1931), Savage (1954), and Jeffrey (1965). But there are dozens of variations on these theorems, and many more indeed for the huge number of non-expected utility theories that have been proposed as descriptive or normative rivals to the orthodox expected utility theory.

I won't attempt to cover all the variety in this section. Instead, I'll start with a brief overview of the main frameworks in which decision-theoretic representations tend to be constructed (Section 6.1), after which I'll go into more detail on (a version of) Ramsey's theorem (Section 6.2). Then I discuss meaningfulness in the conjoint measurement of belief and desire (Section 6.3), and finally rebut some common objections and concerns about the decision-theoretic approach (Section 6.4).

6.1 The Objects of Preference

Before we can build a conjoint representation of preferences as determined by beliefs and desires, we require an appropriate means of formalising the objects over which the preference relation is to be defined. These objects are variably referred to as *gambles*, *bets*, *prospects*, *options*, *acts*, *decisions*, *choices*, and more, depending on the intended interpretation of the theorem and the personal inclinations of its authors. But, broadly speaking, there are three main ways to formalise the objects of preference. These can be roughly ordered by the degree of internal structure they represent those objects as having – that is, from those that posit very richly structured objects of preference to those that define preferences over unstructured sets.

At the 'richly structured' end of the spectrum will be theorems that, like Savage's (1954), employ more or less arbitrary associations between states of nature and consequences. In this context, preferences are usually understood as a relation over actions the agent might perform, or perhaps intentions to perform those actions, with the idea being that actions can be represented by their possible consequences relative to the states of the world under which the action brings them about. Where $S = \{s_1, s_2, \ldots\}$ is a partition of Ω representing different states the world might be in, and $C = \{c_1, c_2, \ldots\}$ is a set of consequences that some potential action could bring about depending on which state happens to be true, we let each action be represented by a function from S to C. (So if f is the function that pairs s_i with c_i, then it represents the action such that were it performed, then if s_1 is the true state then c_1 would result, and if s_2 is the true state then c_2 would result, and so on.) The preference relation is defined over a set of these functions, and a conjoint representation is constructed that (typically, not always) decomposes into two measures – a function on the set of consequences C (corresponding to the desirability of those consequences); and a function on an algebra of propositions (usually called 'events') constructed from the states in S (corresponding to the agent's beliefs).

For example, suppose S is finite, and the set of events $\mathcal{E} = \{e_1, e_2, \ldots\}$ is the algebra of propositions with atoms given by S. Then, an ordinary expected utility theorem provides axioms on a preference relation $\succsim$ defined over the space of actions C^S sufficient for the existence of a probability measure β on $\mathcal{E}$ ('β' for beliefs) and a real-valued function δ on C ('δ' for desires), such that for any actions f and g,

$$f \succsim g \text{ if and only if } \sum_{s \in S} \beta(s)\delta\big(f(s)\big) \geq \sum_{s \in S} \beta(s)\delta\big(g(s)\big).$$

Note that β and δ must here be defined on distinct sets – indeed, in Savage's original construction S and C are disjoint. The reason is that a proposition counts as an event just in case it's logically equivalent to a disjunction of states; hence any proposition that's consistent with any state and its negation cannot be an event. Given that, observe that consequences cannot in general be events, if the functional representation of actions is to be coherent. We cannot say that f is the action that brings consequence c_1 at state s_1, whereas g is the action that brings some other consequence c_2 at s_1, if the state logically determines that a particular consequence obtains. So consequences need to be logically independent of states. For a similar reason, states cannot in general determine actions. Hence, the domain of the belief function cannot include propositions that determine the actions under deliberation nor the consequences thereof. For some this is seen as a good-making feature of Savage's construction (e.g., Spohn 1977); for others, not so much (e.g., Hájek 2016; Elliott 2017a).

At the other end of the spectrum are theorems that, like Jeffrey's (1965; 1978; see also Bolker 1967 and Domotor 1978), define preferences over an algebra of propositions (qua sets of worlds) that simultaneously serves as the domain of both the belief and desire functions. For this reason they are sometimes called 'monoset theorems'. Jeffrey's theorem supplies axioms on a preference relation $\succsim$ defined over an algebra of propositions $\mathcal{A}$ sufficient for the existence of a probability measure β and a real-valued δ where $p \succsim q$ if and only if $\delta(p) \geq \delta(q)$, and for $p \in \mathcal{A}$, if $\{p_1, p_2, \ldots, p_n\}$ is any finite partition of p, then:

$$\delta(p) = \sum_{i=1}^{n} \beta(p_i \mid p)\delta(p_i)$$

It makes little sense to interpret the objects of Jeffrey's preference relation as actions. *Some* of the propositions in $\mathcal{A}$ may very well correspond to actions that the agent may choose to perform – these Jeffrey (1968, 170) refers to as *actual* propositions – but many more of the propositions over which $\succsim$ is defined will correspond to no plausible object of choice in any realistic decision context. So $\succsim$ is much better seen in this case as a relative desirability relation:

> To say that p is ranked higher than q [in the agent's preference ordering] means that the agent would welcome the news that p is true more than he would the news that q is true: p would be better news than q. (Jeffrey 1990, 82)

Given this, the axioms of Jeffrey's theorem constrain the agent's relative desirabilities for propositions in general, and decision-making is construed as selecting between actual propositions on the basis of their desirabilities in contexts where one is able to make one or another of them true.

The difference in how the objects of preference are represented is also important from a measurement-theoretic perspective. For any numerical representation of any weak order, if that representation is going to be more than just an ordinal scale then one needs posit *some* additional structure when characterising the qualitative system – else there will be nothing for the extra-ordinal structure of the representation to be a representation *of*. In the Savage framework, the additional structure can be found mostly in the objects of preference. For example, Savage's theorem requires:

- If $f(s) = c_1$ and $g(s) = c_2$ for all $s \in S$, and $f > g$, then if $f'(s) = g'(s)$ for all $s \in X \subset S$, and otherwise $f'(s) = f(s)$ and $g'(s) = g(s)$, then $f' > g'$.

In other words, if two acts f' and g' have identical consequences for a subset of the states, and for all other states f' has better consequences, then f' should be preferred to g'. In the Jeffrey framework, however, the relata of $\succsim$ have no internal structure; they are just sets of worlds. Hence, we need to appeal instead to logical (or set-theoretic) relations between propositions to get an interesting (more-than-merely-ordinal) representation. For example:

- If $(p \cup q) \sim q$ for some $q \in \mathcal{A}$ such that $p \cap q = \varnothing$ and either $p > q$ or $q > p$, then $(p \cup r) \sim r$ for all $r \in \mathcal{A}$.

In other words, if p makes no contribution to the desirability of $p \cup q$ for disjoint p and q of distinct desirabilities, then the agent must presumably have zero confidence in p, and hence for consistency p should make no contribution to the desirability of $p \cup r$ for any other r.

An interesting middle ground is provided by the third kind of framework, originating with Ramsey (1931), where preferences are defined over a domain of very simple prospects of the form 'c_1 if p, c_2 otherwise'. These are typically interpreted as conjunctions of conditionals, perhaps corresponding to potential choices or gambles the agent might take. They are typically formalised as n-tuples of conditions and consequences – for example, (c_1, p, c_2). Most such theorems focus on binary prospects like the one just described. In some cases preferences are also defined for ternary prospects 'c_1 if p, c_2 if q, c_3 otherwise', or sometimes even quarternary prospects, but nothing so richly structured as the (potentially infinitary) act-functions we find in the Savage-style frameworks. (For examples of theorems in the Ramseyan framework, see Debreu 1959; Davidson & Suppes 1956; Davidson *et al.* 1957; Fishburn 1967; Elliott 2017b; 2017c.) The theorem discussed in the next section belongs to this third class.

It's worth noting that the Ramseyan approach is *extremely* limited as a framework for formalising decision theory – especially in contrast to either of the Savagean or Jeffreyan frameworks just discussed. Most decision situations involve choices between options that cannot plausibly be reduced to simple n-ary prospects, for very small n. Our decisions usually have more than two or three possible consequences. Savage and Jeffrey sought to achieve a complete and fully general axiomatisation of a decision theory in terms of preferences, and from this perspective the Ramseyan framework is grossly inadequate.

But for a *theory of measurement* we needn't ask so much. The goal here is to isolate a qualitative conjoint psychological system with a relational structure that suffices to explain the quantitation of belief. With that in mind, we needn't assume that the qualitative system should include all of the agent's preferences over all possible actions and/ propositions, nor that the decision rule should be generally applicable to every conceivable decision situation.

6.2 Ramsey's Theorem

Here's the goal: from a single preference ordering over a space of binary prospects (e.g, of the form 'c_1 if p, c_2 otherwise'), we want to extract numerical representations of belief and desire that conjointly represent those preferences according to a version of the expected utility rule.

The first step is to be more precise about the form of the intended numerical representation. We let $\succsim$ be a preference relation defined over a set G of prospects. Where $\mathcal{A} = \{p, q, r, \ldots\}$ is an algebra of propositions and $C = \{c_1, c_2, c_3, \ldots\}$ is a set of consequences, we formalise prospects as 3-tuples (c_1, p, c_2) in $G \subseteq C \times \mathcal{A} \times C$.[18] For simplicity, we will be assuming that both $\mathcal{A}$ and C are finite. This just lets us ignore a complicated 'Archimedean' axiom that's trivially satisfied in finite contexts. Given that, we desire a function $\varphi \colon G \mapsto \mathbb{R}$ that represents $\succsim$ in the sense that

$$(c_1, p, c_2) \succsim (c_3, q, c_4) \text{ if and only if } \varphi(c_1, p, c_2) \geq \varphi(c_3, q, c_4),$$

where φ itself decomposes into two functions $\beta \colon \mathcal{A} \mapsto \mathbb{R}$ (for beliefs) and $\delta \colon C \mapsto \mathbb{R}$ (for desires) such that

$$\varphi(c_1, p, c_2) = \delta(c_1)\beta(p) + \delta(c_2)(1 - \beta(p)).$$

Call this the *simplified formula*.

Note an immediate complication: the simplified formula is too simple! It implies that the three factors contributing to the value of a prospect are independent of one another. In particular, according to the simplified formula,

$$\beta(p) = \beta(q) \text{ if and only if } \varphi(c_1, p, c_2) = \varphi(c_1, q, c_2).$$

However, the desirability of c_1 – as supposedly represented by $\delta(c_1)$ – may vary depending on whether it obtains in a context where p is true versus a context where q is true, which could imply a difference in desirability between (c_1, p, c_2) and (c_1, q, c_2). In general, the value of a prospect's consequences ought to be

---

[18] We don't presume that $\mathcal{A}$ and C are disjoint sets, nor that the consequences are maximally specific. In Ramsey's essay, consequences are maximally specific worlds, or in some cases *almost*-worlds that are maximally specific up to a single question about which the agent cares not. With some minor adjustments, this ends up being unnecessary for the representation result and for the decision theory underlying it.

judged relative to the conditions under which those consequences obtain. Consequently, the value of (c_1, p, c_2) *isn't* always given by the simplified formula, but by the slightly more complicated one:

$$\varphi(c_1, p, c_2) = \delta(p \wedge c_1)\beta(p) + \delta(\neg p \wedge c_2)(1 - \beta(p))$$

The implication is that if $\succsim$ is determined by this more complicated decision rule, then *either* it cannot be represented in the desired manner, *or* $\succsim$ cannot be defined for all possible prospects in $C \times \mathcal{A} \times C$. The resolution to this little problem is to restrict G to those prospects (c_1, p, c_2) such that the agent is indifferent between c_1 and $c_1 \wedge p$, and likewise between c_2 and $c_2 \wedge \neg p$, since in these cases the complicated formula will just reduce to the simplified formula. If propositions are coarsely individuated – if they are sets of logically possible worlds, as per **Assumption 1** – then one way to achieve this restriction is to suppose that a prospect can be found in G only if its consequences entail the conditions under which they obtain, so $c_1 = p \wedge c_1$ and $c_2 = \neg p \wedge c_2$. More precisely:

1. $(c_1, p, c_2) \in G$ only if c_1 implies $p \wedge c_1$ and c_2 implies $\neg p \wedge c_2$; and $p \wedge c_1$ is inconsistent only if p is inconsistent, and $\neg p \wedge c_2$ is inconsistent only if $\neg p$ is inconsistent   (*restricted prospects*)

But this only tells us what kinds of prospects *aren't* in G. We will also need to ensure that the domain of $\succsim$ is rich enough to ensure the existence of the desired representation. There are five richness axioms in total, starting with:

2. For every $c \in C$, there is a prospect $(c, p, c) \in G$ (*trivial prospects*)

The purpose of this axiom is to let us extend the preference ordering $\succsim$ to the set of consequences C, in the obvious way:

$$c_1 \succsim c_2 \text{ if and only if } \exists (c_1, p, c_1), (c_2, q, c_2) \in G : (c_1, p, c_1) \succsim (c_2, q, c_2)$$

Axioms 7–10, presented later, will ensure that $\succsim$ on C is a weak order. This *trivial prospects* axiom isn't necessary if we treat preferences over consequences as a primitive relation. That is what Ramsey did. However, letting preferences be defined in the first instance only over gambles, rather than both gambles and their consequences, makes some parts of the construction slightly more natural.

Before I state the four remaining richness axioms, some notation will prove useful. First, let $\underline{c}$ designate the set of consequences c' in C such that $c \sim c'$. In terms of the intended representation, $\underline{c}$ contains all and only those c' such that $\delta(c) = \delta(c')$. We then use $(\underline{c_1}, p, \underline{c_2})$ for a prospect conditional on p

with consequences equal in desirability to c_1 and c_2. Next, suppose that, for $c_1 > c_2$,

$$(\underline{c_1}, p, \underline{c_2}) \gtrsim (\underline{c_1}, q, \underline{c_2}).$$

Supposing $\gtrsim$ is represented in the desired format, this can hold only if $\beta(p) \geq \beta(q)$. Consequently, if

$$(\underline{c_1}, p, \underline{c_2}) \gtrsim (\underline{c_1}, \neg p, \underline{c_2}),$$

then $\beta(p) = \beta(\neg p)$. In this fashion we can isolate the half-probability propositions in $\mathcal{A}$. We use $(\underline{c_1}, \frac{1}{2}, \underline{c_2})$ for a prospect with consequences equal in desirability to c_1 and c_2 conditional on one or another of these half-probability propositions. These prospects can be used to define halfway points between the desirabilities of c_1 and c_2. Finally, we characterise a qualitative ordering $\gtrsim_\Delta$ over $C \times C$ like so:

$$(c_1, c_2) \gtrsim_\Delta (c_3, c_4) \text{ if and only if } (\underline{c_1}, \frac{1}{2}, \underline{c_4}) \gtrsim (\underline{c_2}, \frac{1}{2}, \underline{c_3})$$

Defined as such, $\gtrsim_\Delta$ represents the relative size of *intervals* in desirability – in the final representation, we will see

$$(c_1, c_2) \gtrsim_\Delta (c_3, c_4) \text{ if and only if } \delta(c_1) - \delta(c_2) \geq \delta(c_3) - \delta(c_4).$$

We can now state the remaining richness axioms with comparative ease:

3. If $c_1 > c_2$, then there is some $(\underline{c_1}, \frac{1}{2}, \underline{c_2}) \in G$ *(halfway prospects)*
4. If $(c_1, c_2) \gtrsim_\Delta (c_3, c_4) \gtrsim_\Delta (c_1, c_1)$, then there are $c_5, c_6 \in C$ such that $(c_1, c_5) \sim_\Delta (c_3, c_4) \sim_\Delta (c_6, c_2)$ *(Δ-solvability)*
5. For every $(c_1, p, c_2) \in G$, there's some $(c_3, q, c_3) \in G$ such that $(c_1, p, c_2) \sim (c_3, q, c_3)$, or some $(c_4, \frac{1}{2}, c_5) \in G$ such that $(c_1, p, c_2) \sim (\underline{c_4}, \frac{1}{2}, \underline{c_5})$ *(extendibility)*
6. For every $p \in \mathcal{A}$, there's some $(\underline{c_1}, p, \underline{c_2}) \in G$ such that $c_1 > c_2$ or $c_2 > c_1$ *(non-trivial prospects)*

The *halfway prospects* axiom ensures that we can always define halfway points between the desirabilities of any two consequences. *Δ-solvability* is a non-necessary condition used to guarantee that for any non-zero interval in desirability between two consequences, there will be another interval of the same size to which it can be 'added'. This allows ratios of differences to be defined, which is what ultimately allows the construction of an interval-scale measure δ. The *extendibility* axiom is then used to extend δ on C to all of G, and hence define φ. Finally, *non-trivial prospects* ensures there are enough prospects around such that a degree of belief can be defined for every proposition in $\mathcal{A}$.

Definition 23. Where $\mathcal{A}$ is a finite algebra of propositions and C is a finite set of propositions, $\langle G, \succsim \rangle$ is a *finite Ramseyan structure* if and only if $G \subseteq C \times \mathcal{A} \times C$ satisfying *restricted prospects*, *trivial prospects*, *halfway prospects*, Δ-*solvability*, *extendability* and *non-trivial prospects*.

What remains is to specify conditions on a finite Ramsey structure sufficient for the existence of the desired representation. We proceed in three stages, starting with the construction of the desirability function δ. This uses:

7. $\succsim$ is a weak order   (*weak order*)
8. $\succsim_\Delta$ is transitive   (Δ-*transitivity*)
9. For all $c_1, c_2 \in C$, $(c_1, \frac{1}{2}, c_2) \sim (c_2, \frac{1}{2}, c_1)$ (*reversibility*)
10. For all $c_1, c_2 \in C$, if $c_1 \succsim c_2$, then $(c_1, p, c_1) \succsim (c_1, q, c_2)$ (*averaging*)

In overview, δ is derived as follows. (For details, see Elliott 2017c and Krantz *et al.* 1971, 145–52.) First, we use *weak order*, Δ-*transitivity* and *reversibility*, in conjunction with *halfway prospects* and Δ-*solvability*, to define a concatenation operation $\oplus$ over desirability intervals, such that $\langle C \times C, \succsim_\Delta; \oplus \rangle$ is an additive extensive structure. This allows for a ratio-scale measure of desirability intervals. Given *averaging*, we can define an interval-scale measure $\delta : C \mapsto \mathbb{R}$ such that:

  i. $c_1 \succsim c_2$ if and only if $\delta(c_1) \geq \delta(c_2)$
  ii. $(c_1, c_2) \succsim_\Delta (c_3, c_4)$ if and only if $\delta(c_1) - \delta(c_2) \geq \delta(c_3) - \delta(c_4)$

Next, we define φ on G using δ, like so:

$$\varphi(c_1, p, c_2) = \begin{cases} \delta(c_3) & \text{if } (c_1, p, c_2) \sim (c_3, q, c_3) \\ \frac{1}{2}(\delta(c_3) - \delta(c_4)) & \text{if } c_3 >_\delta c_4 \text{ and } (c_1, p, c_2) \sim (c_3, \frac{1}{2}, c_4) \end{cases}$$

The *extendibility* axiom ensures the definition is adequate. Note, of course, that $\delta(c) = \varphi(c, p, c)$. Finally, we extract the belief function β out of φ. Where $c_1 > c_2$, reorganising the simplified formula gets us $\beta(p)$ as a ratio of differences in desirability:

$$\beta(p) = \frac{\varphi(c_1, p, c_2) - \delta(c_2)}{\delta(c_1) - \delta(c_2)}$$

This last step requires the *non-trivial prospects* axiom, plus one more axiom which asserts that the contribution $\beta(p)$ makes to the overall value of a prospect is independent of the desirabilities of its consequences. Expressed directly in terms of preferences, this axiom is rather complicated and not at all intuitive. The interested reader should refer to Davidson and Suppes' (1956) axiom A10 and the associated definitions for how it goes. We can simplify matters greatly by 'cheating' and expressing the axiom in terms of the intended representation:

11. For all $p \in \mathcal{A}$, if $\delta(c_1) \neq \delta(c_2)$, $\delta(c_3) \neq \delta(c_4)$, and $(c_1, p, c_2), (c_3, p, c_4) \in \mathcal{G}$, then

$$\frac{\varphi(c_1, p, c_2) - \delta(c_2)}{\delta(c_1) - \delta(c_2)} = \frac{\varphi(c_3, p, c_4) - \delta(c_4)}{\delta(c_3) - \delta(c_4)}$$

(*independence*)

The upshot is that the foregoing definition of $\beta(p)$ won't depend on the particular choice of prospect. It is a consistency requirement, on how the agent values different prospects conditional on the same proposition.

Putting that all together:

Theorem 24 Ramsey (1931); Elliott (2017c) *If $\langle \mathcal{G}, \succsim \rangle$ is a finite Ramseyan structure satisfying weak order, Δ-transitivity, reversibility, averaging, and independence, then there are functions $\varphi: \mathcal{G} \mapsto \mathbb{R}$, $\delta: C \mapsto \mathbb{R}$ and $\beta: \mathcal{A} \mapsto \mathbb{R}$, such that*

    i. $(c_1, p, c_2) \succsim (c_3, q, c_4)$ *if and only if* $\varphi(c_1, p, c_2) \geq \varphi(c_3, q, c_4)$

    ii. $\varphi(c_1, p, c_2) = \delta(c_1)\beta(p) + \delta(c_2)(1 - \beta(p))$

Furthermore, δ is unique up to a positive affine transformation, while β is unique and for all $p \in \mathcal{A}$,

    iii. $1 \geq \beta(p) = 1 - \beta(\neg p) \geq 0$.

Note that β is unique *simpliciter* – an absolute scale. The uniqueness clause applies to all representations satisfying properties i and ii. (Property iii, by contrast, is not an explicit stipulation on the form of the representation but is rather derived as a consequence of the representation.) The uniqueness of β is a result of how it was defined – as a dimensionless ratio of differences in desirability – and the fact that δ is unique up to an interval-preserving transformation.

6.3 Uniqueness and Meaning

It's a point often noted that the expected utility representations of a preference ordering are not unique. Theorem 24 implies, for example, that if $\succsim$ has an expected utility representation involving the pair of belief and desire functions

β and δ, then there will be another such representation involving β and $\delta^\star$, where

$$\delta^\star(c) = 9\delta(c) + 1.$$

Since it's widely held that desirabilities can be measured on nothing stronger than an interval scale (similar to temperatures as measured in Celsius or Fahrenheit), the usual response to this fact is that there is no meaningful difference between δ and $\delta^\star$.

Now consider the following example, from Zynda (2000). Where γ is an n-ary prospect with consequences $\gamma(p_i)$ conditional on which element of a partition $p_1, \ldots, p_n$ happens to be true, then $\succsim$ has an expected utility representation involving β and δ whenever $\gamma \succsim \gamma'$ if and only if

$$\sum_{i=1}^{n} \beta(p_i)\delta\big(\gamma(p_i)\big) \geq \sum_{i=1}^{n} \beta(p_i)\delta\big(\gamma'(p_i)\big).$$

If any such representation exists, then there will be another representation of $\succsim$ involving the functions $\beta^\star$ and δ, where

$$\beta^\star(p) = 9\beta(p) + 1.$$

In this case, though, the belief and desire functions will be combined by a different decision rule – the *valuation maximisation rule*. This rule tells us that $\gamma \succsim \gamma'$ just in case

$$\sum_{i=1}^{n} \beta^\star(p_i)\delta\big(\gamma(p_i)\big) - \delta\big(\gamma(p_i)\big) \geq \sum_{i=1}^{n} \beta^\star(p_i)\delta\big(\gamma'(p_i)\big) - \delta\big(\gamma'(p_i)\big).$$

It is straightforward to show that an expected utility representation of $\succsim$ (with β and δ) exists if and only if a valuation maximisation representation of $\succsim$ (with $\beta^\star$ and δ) likewise exists. The key step is then just to note that the transformation from β to $\beta^\star$ is bijective and so invertible:

$$\beta(p) = \frac{\beta^\star(p) - 1}{9}.$$

So, substituting into the inequality for expected utility representations just presented:

$$\sum_{i=1}^{n} \left(\frac{\beta^\star(p_i) - 1}{9}\right)\delta\big(\gamma(p_i)\big) \geq \sum_{i=1}^{n} \left(\frac{\beta^\star(p_i) - 1}{9}\right)\delta\big(\gamma'(p_i)\big).$$

Then dropping the constant factor:

$$\sum_{i=1}^{n} \left(\beta^{\star}(p_i) - 1\right)\delta\left(\gamma(p_i)\right) \geq \sum_{i=1}^{n} \left(\beta^{\star}(p_i) - 1\right)\delta\left(\gamma'(p_i)\right),$$

which is just another way to write the valuation maximisation rule.

By analogy with desirabilities, one might imagine this tells us something about meaningfulness in β and $\beta^{\star}$: that in just the same way as we wanted to say that δ and $\delta^{\star}$ are not meaningfully distinct, so too should we want to say that β and $\beta^{\star}$ are not meaningfully distinct. As Zynda (2000) has suggested,

> One might point out that $\beta^{\star}$ is simply a linear transformation of β, and argue that in the case of probabilities (like utilities and temperatures) this is a difference that makes no difference. This approach commits [the theorist] to taking as real properties of degrees of belief at most those properties that are common to *both* (p. 64)

And a little further on, Zynda argues that β and $\beta^{\star}$ will share a common ordering, and thus represent the same comparative confidences. Hence,

> According to this solution, people really have properties that can properly be called 'degrees of belief', though these are more abstract in nature than subjective probabilities, being purely qualitative ... the concept of degree of belief on this strategy becomes a *purely ordinal notion*. (p. 65, emphasis added)

However, while there *is* an important lesson about meaningfulness to be gleaned from this example, this is not it.

First note that β and $\beta^{\star}$ will have more than just their orderings in common. The linear transformation which relates β to $\beta^{\star}$ also preserves difference ratios, and those ratios are not decision-theoretically superfluous. Again, the example from Section 3.4 suffices to make this point. Where $\mathcal{A} = \{\Omega, p, \neg p, \varnothing\}$, we imagine that Ramsey has a choice between:

α: receive \$1 if p is true, nothing otherwise
β: receive \$2 if p is false, nothing otherwise

According to expected utility theory, Ramsey should prefer α if and only if

$$\frac{\beta(\Omega) - \beta(\varnothing)}{\beta(p) - \beta(\varnothing)} < \frac{\beta(p) - \beta(\varnothing)}{\beta(\neg p) - \beta(\varnothing)}.$$

As there are numerically distinct but ordinally equivalent probability measures that differ with respect to this inequality, expected utility theory requires that there are meaningful differences between those measures. The same is therefore true for the valuation maximisation rule, according to which Ramsey should prefer α if and only if

$$\frac{\beta^\star(\Omega) - \beta^\star(\varnothing)}{\beta^\star(p) - \beta^\star(\varnothing)} < \frac{\beta^\star(p) - \beta^\star(\varnothing)}{\beta^\star(\neg p) - \beta^\star(\varnothing)}.$$

Do not be tempted, though, to infer from these facts that difference ratios are meaningful in β. (They *are* meaningful; the mistake is to think the reason has anything to do with what's common to β and $\beta^\star$.) For consider yet another decision-theoretic representation. Define $\beta^\dagger$ such that

$$\beta^\dagger(p) = \beta^\star(p)^2.$$

Now $\succsim$ has an expected utility representation involving β and δ if and only if it also has an 'equivalent' *schmaluation maximisation* representation involving $\beta^\dagger$ and δ, where this time we say $\gamma \succsim \gamma'$ if and only if

$$\sum_{i=1}^{n} \left(\sqrt{\overline{\beta^\dagger(p_i)}} - 1 \right) \delta(\gamma(p_i)) \geq \sum_{i=1}^{n} \left(\sqrt{\beta^\dagger(p_i)} - 1 \right) \delta(\gamma'(p_i)).$$

However, difference ratios are *not* preserved in the transformation from β to $\beta^\dagger$. So if earlier we were tempted to say that difference ratios are meaningful in β only if they're shared with $\beta^\star$, then by the same token they should be shared with $\beta^\dagger$ as well – but then difference ratios wouldn't be meaningful after all.

The proof that a schmaluation maximisation representation exists just in case an expected utility representation exists is near identical to that for the valuation maximisation representations presented earlier, and relies mostly on the fact that the transformation from β to $\beta^\dagger$ is bijective and so invertible:

$$\beta(p) = \frac{\sqrt{\beta^\dagger(p)} - 1}{9}.$$

And it generalises easily: if the transformation from β to $\beta^\dagger$ is bijective, then we'll be able to construct a representation of $\succsim$ which makes use of β^x and δ, where that representation exists if and only if an expected utility representation with β and δ exists. This includes transformations that do not preserve ratios, or difference ratios, or even orderings. In fact, there's virtually nothing that's shared across all possible decision-theoretic representations of $\succsim$. But it would be a gross error to infer that almost all the information in β is meaningless.

Clearly, whether something is meaningful in β has nothing much to do with what kind of information β shares or doesn't share with $\beta^\star$ and $\beta^\dagger$. And hopefully you can see the problem: the valuation and schmaluation maximisation representations are 'equivalent' to the expected utility representation in the sense that they are equally legitimate ways to numerically represent a system of preferences, but they are representations *within distinct numerical systems* – and *meaningfulness* in the representation of any quantity is only sensibly defined relative to a fixed choice of numerical format (§2.5). Indeed, for any real-valued representation φ of any quantity, if φ and φ' are related by an invertible transformation on the reals, then φ' will *also* be a way of representing that quantity *in some numerical system or other*. This includes transformations that do not preserve ratios, or difference ratios, or even orderings.

What Zynda-style examples actually establish is that ratios in β *are* meaningful *relative to* expected utility representations, precisely because any transformation of β that doesn't preserve ratios must therefore employ a different combination rule. Since ratios are meaningful, therefore difference ratios and orderings are also meaningful. But there is a deeper lesson here too: the *conjoint* structure being represented isn't any structure *internal* to the system of beliefs itself, considered in isolation from anything else, but relates instead to the connection between beliefs, desires, and preferences. The belief functions β, $\beta^\star$, and $\beta^\dagger$ do have *something* in common – they all play similar roles in the respective numerical models of decision-making that employ them. (Essentially: *these* beliefs interact with *those* desires to produce such-and-such preferences.) *That* is what's invariant, and that is why we cannot transform the belief function without making adjustments to the decision rule: because the *meaning* of β is tied up with how it interacts with δ to produce preferences. Of course there are many ways to represent that conjoint system – there are always many ways to represent any system. But however we do so, the three components of the representation – the belief function, the desire function, and the decision rule – need to be interpreted together.

For an analogy, consider the relationship between force, mass, and acceleration. If those quantities are represented in Newtons, kilograms, and metres per second squared (respectively), then the connection between them can be neatly captured with the usual formula:

$$F = ma.$$

But if we start playing around with the numerical representation of the different components, then we can easily come up with many numerically distinct but 'equivalent' representations of the very same relationship. Where mass is measured in pounds, acceleration in schmetres per second squared,[19] and force in negative Newtons, then we get:

$$F = \frac{-5m \cdot \log_2(a)}{11}.$$

---

[19] Recall from Section 2.4 that the schmetre is a multiplicative variant of the metre, defined such that n metres is 2^n schmetres.

The superficial form of the rule has changed, but not the underlying relational system between the three quantities. What's happening with the different ways of expressing the connection between beliefs, desires, and preferences is no different in kind than what's happening with these different ways of expressing the connection between force, mass, and acceleration.

6.4 An Apology

Theorem 24 describes a very flexible representation of belief – β must be such that $\beta(p) \in [0, 1]$ and $\beta(p) = 1 - \beta(\neg p)$, but otherwise there are few constraints on the shape it must take. It's possible to construct finite Ramseyan structures such that β is logically non-omniscient, and it's also possible to construct finite Ramseyan structures such that β is a probability measure. Given the desiderata of Section 3.4, I take it that this flexibility is a good-making feature. It allows for a non-disjunctive theory of belief measurement that's consistent with a range of probabilistic and non-probabilistic representations, on a more-than-merely ordinal scale, without forcing logical omniscience.

The reason for this flexibility is that the degree of belief assigned to p is determined independently of almost any other proposition, aside from $\neg p$. This contrasts with epistemic approaches (and Jeffrey-style decision-theoretic approaches). The quantitation of belief on the Ramseyan approach requires no particular appeal to relations between belief states or the contents thereof, but instead depends primarily on systematic relationships between the agent's degree of belief in p and the value they attach to prospects conditional on p. As Ramsey (1931) put it,

> [The] degree of a belief is a causal property of it, which we can express vaguely as the extent to which we are prepared to act on it. (p. 169)

A rough way to express the difference: on the epistemic approach, the strength of Sally's belief towards p is twice that of q when p is equiprobable with the disjunction of two incompatible q' and q'' equiprobable with q; on the Ramseyan approach, if p is believed to twice the degree as q, then this will be connected to the difference in desirability between (c_1, p, c_2) and c_2 being twice the difference between (c_1, q, c_2) and c_2 (for $c_1 > c_2$).

It's worth emphasising again that the connection between belief and preference needn't be *constitutive*. Many have claimed to find in Ramsey's essay the thesis that beliefs are nothing over and above preferences as manifest in choice dispositions. Ramsey himself never said that, and instead characterised the relationship between them in causal terms. But in any case, nothing about

Theorem 24 implies that beliefs are *reducible* to preferences. It's true that in the proof of the theorem we first characterise a desirability function that represents preferences and from that go on to derive a belief function – but one cannot infer any kind of ontological or conceptual dependence relations between quantities just from the order in which their numerical representations happen to be constructed in a conjoint representation thereof. That would be fallacious. The numerical representation requires a qualitative interpretation involving *some* systematic connection between beliefs and preferences, but that connection may take many possible forms.

Recognising this fallacy helps in dealing with some common objections to the decision-theoretic approach. An exemplar here is Eriksson and Hájek's (2007) Zen monk. A 'Zen monk' is an agent who is indifferent between all consequences, and therefore indifferent between all prospects. The preferences of such an agent would violate *non-trivial prospects* in such a way that the belief function β cannot be derived from the agents' desirabilities. Yet, presumably, such an agent could still have determinate degrees of belief, and two Zen monks could have distinct degrees of belief between them. If such beings could exist, then they are a counterexample to the thesis that an agent's degrees of belief are nothing over and above their preferences. But the Zen monk is much less problematic if we take the strength of an agent's belief to be 'a causal property of it' which need not be manifest in all cases (Elliott 2019a). Even if a Zen monk is actually indifferent among all consequences, she may still be in a state of belief the typical causal role of which would only become apparent if she were no longer universally indifferent. What it is to believe p to degree x, on this picture, is to be in a state whose typical causal role in connection to preferences and desire is reflected in the class of systems with representations such that $\beta(p) = x$.

Another common objection is that Ramsey's theorem (and the like) only establishes conditions under which a preference relation behaves *as if* it's determined by such-and-such beliefs and desires combined according to the expected utility rule – it doesn't guarantee that the agent *really has* those beliefs and desires (cf. Zynda 2000; Christensen 2001; Eriksson & Hájek 2007; Meacham & Weisberg 2011). The observation is correct, of course, just as it would also be correct to say that a representation theorem for the conjoint measurement of momentum as determined by mass and velocity only supplies conditions under which momentum behaves *as if* it's determined by mass and velocity. But so what? If the point of a decision-theoretic representation theorem were to show that an agent whose preferences satisfy the axioms must therefore have the beliefs and desires they are represented as having, then it would be safe to say that no such theorem has ever succeeded in that task. It's not the sort of thing they *can* show. Lucky, then, that this isn't the only way to interpret Theorem 24!

A much more fruitful interpretation is in terms of measurement. The aptness of the conjoint representation is *presupposed* as part of the theoretical background on which the account of measurement is founded, not magically derived from the representation theorem. Ramsey (1931) knew this:

> I propose to take as a basis a general psychological theory, which ... comes, I think, fairly close to the truth in the sorts of cases with which we are most concerned. I mean the theory that we act in the way we think most likely to realize the objects of our desires, so that a person's actions are completely determined by his desires and opinions. (p. 173)

What Ramsey's theorem supplies is an explanation of the quantitation of belief and desire in the context of that model of decision-making. There's nothing unusual about this – the quantitation of any quantity is always explained against a backdrop of theoretical models and presuppositions.

So we shouldn't be worried about that objection. However, a natural followup concern is that the expected utility model of decision making is unrealistic – and if that's the case, then the qualitative systems these models represent may fail to capture any explanatorily relevant relations at all. Addressing this concern will take a little more work, since the response depends on where the lack of realism originates. There are two main sources, which I'll discuss in turn.

The first is the extremely precise nature of the numerical representation – it involves real-valued degrees of belief and desire, combined with perfect consistency according to a precise decision rule. To achieve such a precise representation, we require strong assumptions about the richness of the domain over which the preferences are defined and about the structure of the preferences over that domain. That's hardly surprising – infinite precision is a strong property for a representation to have. For the same reason, I do not think we should be too concerned with any lack of realism arising from this source. Such is an inevitable consequence of trying to model a squishy psychological system in a rigid numerical framework, and any feasible theory of belief measurement needs to allow for some idealisations that make the topic tractable. It's enough if the systems we characterise are in the ballpark of realism. More importantly, it's usually possible to isolate and weaken or remove the axioms (or parts of the axioms) that are required in fixing the precision of the representation, if we're willing to accept somewhat weaker uniqueness conditions as a result.

I said 'somewhat weaker' for a reason. Critics of decision-theoretic representation theorems tend to write as though failing to establish a *unique* real-valued belief function is the same as establishing no bounds on degrees of belief at all – as if any lack-of-uniqueness implies radical non-uniqueness. More often, though, one can weaken the very strong axioms required for unique real-valued representation and while still establishing tight bounds on that representation. Consider some examples. I've already talked about how the *weak order* axiom can be replaced with a weaker *preorder* axiom so as to allow for incompleteness, leading to a representation of 'imprecise' beliefs and desires (Section 3.3). So consider instead the *extendibility* axiom. This (structural) axiom helps us to pinpoint precise degrees of belief by fixing a precise φ-value for some appropriate prospect (c_1, p, c_2) conditional on p; it does so either by setting that value equal to the desirability of a consequence or equal to the midway point between two consequences. But where *extendibility* is violated and the required prospects don't exist, we can still characterise bounds on degrees of belief provided there are c_3, c_4 such that

$$c_1 \gtrsim c_3 > (c_1, p, c_2) > c_4 \gtrsim c_2.$$

In this case, the value of $\beta(p)$ will be bound like so:

$$\frac{\delta(c_1) - \delta(c_3)}{\delta(c_1) - \delta(c_2)} > \beta(p) > \frac{\delta(c_1) - \delta(c_4)}{\delta(c_1) - \delta(c_2)}$$

More or less the same effect can be achieved if the *independence* axiom is violated. That axiom requires perfect consistency across how every prospect conditional on p is evaluated relative to its consequences, which is necessary if $\beta(p)$ is to be defined as a ratio of differences in real-valued desirabilities. But it's possible to weaken *independence* to allow for a bit of fuzziness in the evaluation of prospects, with corresponding fuzziness in the characterisation of β. Essentially, where the axiom is violated then for every p there's still a unique – and potentially very narrow – interval $[x, y]$ such that every prospect on p is valued as if $\beta(p) \in [x, y]$.

In like fashion we can define bounds on the desirabilities of consequences where any or all of *trivial gambles*, *halfway prospects*, and/or *Δ-solvability* are violated. In general, the point here is that some of the axioms (or some parts of some axioms) in a decision-theoretic representation theorem primarily serve to ensure a *precise* numerical representation – and while they tend to be quite unrealistic, it is not so hard to weaken them. The effect of doing so is a little less precision in the numbers obtained, but nothing more substantially affecting the basic explanatory structure being represented. I suspect Ramsey (1931) understood this point well, and was expressing as much when he wrote:

I have not worked out the mathematical logic of this in detail, because this would, I think, be rather like working out to seven places of decimals a result only valid to two. (p. 180)

That, I think, is the right attitude. It's not realistic to suppose that degrees of belief (and desire) have all the precision of the real numbers. However, we gain some insight into their quantitation by pretending otherwise, and lose nothing of great import in the fiction.

The second source of potential irrealism will be the more fundamental structure of the expected utility model itself – even after accounting for imprecision in degrees of belief and desirability. Perhaps we do not simply evaluate prospects by weighing the values of its consequences against our confidence that those consequences will obtain, but instead also take risk into account in a manner that *cannot* properly be captured by the expected utility rule (or any 'equivalent' decision rule). If so, then again there is a concern that the model fails to capture any explanatorily relevant relations between beliefs and preferences. We're looking for those relations in the wrong place, because we've been presupposing the wrong psychological picture.

We must be a little careful here. Suppose that ordinary decision-makers systematically violate the expected utility rule when evaluating prospects. Still, that rule may serve as a rational ideal, and Theorem 24 may still prove useful in explaining the quantitation of belief by reference to the role one's beliefs regarding p ought to play in connection to how they *ought* to evaluate prospects conditional on p. I said earlier that we don't have to interpret the systematic relationship between belief and preference that explains the conjoint quantitation thereof as a *constitutive* relation; we don't have to interpret it as a *descriptive* relation either. Similarly, an analytic functionalist might say that the expected utility rule captures the essence of folk psychology (*a la* Lewis 1974), and hence a theorem like Ramsey's can help explain how beliefs are quantitated *according to folk psychology*. Since it's no commitment of analytic functionalism that folk psychology provides a perfect descriptive account of decision-making, concerns about the adequacy of expected utility theory are largely irrelevant to this interpretation. The theory is uncontroversially *close* to the truth in either case, and the analytic functionalist needs nothing stronger than this.

Still, one may be concerned that the expected utility rule is neither descriptively nor normatively adequate, and may not be satisfied with the analytic functionalist's interpretation. In that case, we will need a theory of quantitation formulated against the backdrop of some alternative to expected utility theory. Not to worry, for there are many essentially similar theorems for a wide range of these alternatives. The details change, but in outline the general approach to explaining the quantitation of belief remains more or less the same.

Representation theorems for the huge number of non-expected utility theories are too numerous to discuss in detail, but it's worth looking at one example – Kahneman and Tversky's (1979) prospect theory.[20] I'll start by describing the theory. We designate a special (non-)consequence the *status quo*; in the representation, the desirability of the status quo will be fixed at zero, hence we'll label it '0'. We then focus in on ternary prospects of the form 'c_1 if p, c_2 if q, and 0 otherwise', where p and q are mutually exclusive. We assume that degrees of belief are values between zero and one that sum to one for sets of mutually exclusive and jointly exhaustive propositions. Fixing the desirability of the status quo at zero, according to the expected utility rule:

$$\varphi(c_1, p, c_2, q, 0) = \beta(p)\delta(c_1) + \beta(q)\delta(c_2).$$

In other words, the part of the prospect corresponding to the status quo makes no contribution to the value of the prospect, which is a weighted average of the desirabilities of the remaining consequences. According to prospect theory, however, the weights aren't given by the agent's degrees of belief directly. Instead they're given by a *decision weight* corresponding to the agent's beliefs in combination with their attitudes towards risk, where the latter modify the impact the agent's degrees of belief have on the overall value of a gamble. Where $\pi : [0, 1] \mapsto [0, 1]$ and $\pi(0) = 0$ and $\pi(1) = 1$,

$$\varphi(c_1, p, c_2, 0) = \pi(\beta(p))\delta(c_1) + \pi(\beta(q))\delta(c_2).$$

For example, suppose $\beta(p) = \beta(q) = \frac{1}{2}$, $\delta(c_1) > \delta(c_2)$, and that $\delta(c_3)$ is halfway between $\delta(c_1)$ and $\delta(c_2)$. According to expected utility theory, the desirability of $(c_1, p, c_2, q, 0)$ should be halfway between the desirabilities of c_1 and c_2, so equal to the desirability of c_3. However, if $\pi(\frac{1}{2}) < \frac{1}{2}$, then according to prospect theory the desirability of $(c_1, p, c_2, q, 0)$ will be less than that of c_3. In this case, the decision weight reflects a 'risk averse' attitude whereby the agent would prefer a guaranteed c_3 to a risky prospect with an expected value equal to c_3.

For our purposes, the thing to note is the close similarity between the expected utility formula for evaluating (c_1, p, c_2) and prospect theory's formula

---

[20] I highlight this example because (i) it's simple, (ii) prospect theory is well-known among descriptive theories, and (iii) it's formally similar to expected utility theory's main contemporary normative contender: risk-weighted utility theory (Buchak 2013).

for evaluating $(c_1, p, c_2, q, 0)$. Suppose $q = \neg p$; then in both cases we're looking for a pair of functions, θ and δ, such that the value of the prospect is given by

$$\theta(p)\delta(c_1) + \theta(\neg p)\delta(c_2).$$

The difference between them is that, for expected utility theory, θ is interpreted as the agent's *degrees of belief*; whereas for prospect theory θ is interpreted as a *decision weight* that reflects the agent's degrees of belief and their attitudes towards risk.[21] Thus is it possible, as Kahneman and Tversky observe (1979, 280), to infer decision weights from preferences over simple prospects in a manner that's not dissimilar from how we go about inferring degrees of belief in the original Ramseyan approach. Moreover, and with the appropriate additional axioms on preference, those decision weights can in turn be decomposed into a belief function and a risk function (e.g., Wakker 2004).

The end result is only a light modification on the Ramseyan theme: the degree of a belief is not quite a measure of the extent to which we are prepared to act on it, but instead a measure of the extent we're prepared to act on it *given* our attitudes towards risk. Either way, the meaning of the numerical representation of belief is manifest in the role that representation plays in a decision-theoretic context, and such representations tend to play very much the same kind of role regardless of the precise details of the decision theory in question. Expected utility theory may be unrealistic in some ways, or it may not be, but that doesn't mean the theory of quantitation we get out of it isn't fundamentally on the right track.

---

[21] I'm simplifying, but only a little bit. Another difference between expected utility theory and prospect theory is that decision weights needn't sum to one, so we need slightly more general axioms to represent prospect theory.

References

Alon, S. and E. Lehrer (2014). Subjective multi-prior probability: A representation of a partial likelihood relation. *Journal of Economic Theory 151*(C), 476–92.

Alon, S. and D. Schmeidler (2014). Purely subjective maxmin expected utility. *Journal of Economic Theory 152*, 382–412.

Augustin, T., F. Coolen, G. Cooman, and M. Troffaes (Eds.) (2014). *Introduction to Imprecise Probabilities*. Wiley.

Baccelli, J. (2020). Beyond the metrological viewpoint. *Studies in History and Philosophy of Science Part A 80*, 56–61.

Bolker, E. (1967). A simultaneous axiomatization of utility and subjective probability. *Philosophy of Science 34*(4), 333–40.

Borsboom, D. (2005). *Measuring the Mind: Conceptual Issues in Contemporary Psychometrics*. Cambridge University Press.

Brickhill, H. and L. Horsten (2018). Triangulating non-Archimedean probability. *Review of Symbolic Logic 11*(3), 519–46.

Buchak, L. (2013). *Risk and Rationality*. Oxford University Press.

Builes, D., S. Horowitz, and M. Schoenfield (2022). Dilating and contracting arbitrarily. *Nous 56*(1), 3–20.

Bunge, M. (1973). On confusing 'measure' with 'measurement' in the methodology of behavioral science. In *The Methodological Unity of Science*, pp. 105–22. D. Reidel Publishing.

Chalmers, D. (2011). The nature of epistemic space. In A. Egan and B. Weatherson (Eds.), *Epistemic Modality*, pp. 60–107. Oxford University Press.

Christensen, D. (2001). Preference-based arguments for probabilism. *Philosophy of Science 68*(3), 356–76.

Clark, S. (2000). The measurement of qualitative probability. *Journal of Mathematical Psychology 44*(3), 464–79.

Davidson, D. and P. Suppes (1956). A finitistic axiomatization of subjective probability and utility. *Econometrica 24*(3), 264–75.

Davidson, D., P. Suppes, and S. Siegel (1957). *Decision Making: An Experimental Approach*. Stanford University Press.

de Finetti, B. (1931). Sul significato soggettivo della probabilita. *Fundamenta Mathematicae 17*(1), 298–329.

Debreu, G. (1959). Cardinal utility for even-chance mixtures of pairs of sure prospects. *The Review of Economic Studies 28*(3), 174–7.

Decoene, S., P. Onghena, and R. Janssen (1995). Representationalism under attack: Review of an introduction to the logic of psychological measurement. *Journal of Mathematical Psychology 39*(2), 234–42.

DiBella, N. (2018). The qualitative paradox of non-conglomerability. *Synthese 195*(3), 1181–210.

Domotor, Z. (1970). Qualitative information and entropy structures. In J. Hintikka and P. Suppes (Eds.), *Information and Inference*, pp. 148–94. Reidel.

Domotor, Z. (1978). Axiomatization of Jeffrey utilities. *Synthese 39*(2), 165–210.

Elliott, E. (2017a). Probabilism, representation theorems, and whether deliberation crowds out prediction. *Erkenntnis 82*(2), 379–99.

Elliott, E. (2017b). Ramsey without ethical neutrality: A new representation theorem. *Mind 126*(501), 1–51.

Elliott, E. (2017c). A representation theorem for frequently irrational agents. *Journal of Philosophical Logic 46*(5), 467–506.

Elliott, E. (2019a). Betting against the Zen monk. *Synthese 198*(4), 3733–58.

Elliott, E. (2019b). Impossible worlds and partial belief. *Synthese 196*(8), 3433–58.

Ellis, B. (1968). *Basic Concepts of Measurement Theory*. Cambridge University Press.

Eriksson, L. and A. Hájek (2007). What are degrees of belief? *Studia Logica 86*(2), 183–213.

Evren, O. and E. Ok (2011). On the multi-utility representation of preference relations. *Journal of Mathematical Economics 47*(4–5), 554–63.

Fine, T. (1973). *Theories of Probability: An Examination of Foundations*. Academic Press.

Fishburn, P. (1967). Preference-based definitions of subjective probability. *The Annals of Mathematical Statistics 38*(6), 1605–17.

Hájek, A. (2003). What conditional probability could not be. *Synthese 137*(3), 273–323.

Hájek, A. (2016). Deliberation welcomes prediction. *Episteme 13*(4), 507–28.

Halpern, J. (2001). Lexicographic probability, conditional probability, and nonstandard probability. In *Proceedings of the 8th Conference on Theoretical Aspects of Rationality and Knowledge*, pp. 17–30. Morgan Kaufmann Publishers.

Hawthorne, J. (2016). A logic of comparative support: Qualitative conditional probability relations representable by Popper functions. In A. Hájek and C. Hitchcock (Eds.), *Oxford Handbook of Probabilities and Philosophy*, pp. 277–95. Oxford University Press.

Hölder, O. (1901). Die Axiome der Quantitat und die Lehre vom Mass. *Berichte über die Verhandlungen der Königlich-Sáchsischen Gesellschaft der Wissenschaften zu Leipzig, Mathematisch-Physische Klasse 53*, 1–63.

Jeffrey, R. (1965). *The Logic of Decision*. McGraw-Hill.

Jeffrey, R. (1968). Probable knowledge. *Studies in Logic and the Foundations of Mathematics 51*, 166–90.

Jeffrey, R. (1978). Axiomatizing the logic of decision. In *Foundations and Applications of Decision Theory*, pp. 227–31. Springer.

Jeffrey, R. (1990). *The Logic of Decision (Second Edition)*. University of Chicago Press.

Joyce, J. (2010). A defense of imprecise credences in inference and decision making. *Philosophical Perspectives 24*(1), 281–323.

Kahneman, D. and A. Tversky (1979). Prospect theory: An analysis of decision under risk. *Econometrica 47*(2), 263–91.

Kaplan, M. (2010). In defense of modest probabilism. *Synthese 176*(1), 41–55.

Kaplan, M. and T. Fine (1977). Joint orders in comparative probability. *The Annals of Probability 5*(2), 161–79.

Koopman, B. (1940a). The axioms and algebra of intuitive probability. *Annals of Mathematics 41*(2), 269–92.

Koopman, B. (1940b). The bases of probability. *Bulletin of the American Mathematical Society 46*(10), 763–74.

Kraft, C., J. Pratt, and A. Seidenberg (1959). Intuitive probability on finite sets. *The Annals of Mathematical Statistics 30*(2), 408–19.

Krantz, D., R. Luce, P. Suppes, and A. Tversky (1971). *Foundations of Measurement, Vol. I: Additive and Polynomial Representations*. Academic Press.

Kyburg, H. (1984). *Theory and Measurement*. Cambridge University Press.

Lewis, D. (1974). Radical interpretation. *Synthese 27*(3), 331–44.

Lewis, D. (1979). Attitudes de dicto and de se. *The Philosophical Review 88*(4), 513–43.

Lewis, D. (1986). *On the Plurality of Worlds*. Cambridge University Press.

Luce, D. R. (1968). On the numerical representation of qualitative conditional probability. *The Annals of Mathematical Statistics 39*(2), 481–91.

Luce, R. (1978). Dimensionally invariant numerical laws correspond to meaningful qualitative relations. *Philosophy of Science 45*(1), 1–16.

Luce, R., D. Krantz, P. Suppes, and A. Tversky (1990). *Foundations of Measurement, Vol. III: Representation, Axiomatization, and Invariance*. Dover.

Luce, R. and L. Narens (1978). Qualitative independence in probability theory. *Theory and Decision 9*(3), 225–39.

Luce, R. and J. Tukey (1964). Simultaneous conjoint measurement: A new scale type of fundamental measurement. *Journal of Mathematical Psychology 1*(1), 1–27.

Mari, L. (2005). The problem of foundations of measurement. *Measurement 38*(4), 259–66.

Mari, L., P. Carbone, A. Giordani, and D. Petri (2017). A structural interpretation of measurement and some related epistemological issues. *Studies in History and Philosophy of Science 65–66*, 46–56.

Mayo-Wilson, C. and G. Wheeler (2019). Epistemic decision theory's reckoning. Manuscript. http://philsci-archive.pitt.edu/16374/1/25a_EDTR.pdf.

Meacham, C., and J. Weisberg (2011). Representation theorems and the foundations of decision theory. *Australasian Journal of Philosophy 89*(4), 641–63.

Michell, J. (2021). Representational measurement theory: Is its number up? *Theory & Psychology 31*, 3–23.

Mundy, B. (1987). The metaphysics of quantity. *Philosophical Studies 51*, 29–54.

Mundy, B. (1994). Quantity, representation and geometry. In P. Humphries (Ed.), *Patrick Suppes: Scientific Philosopher*, pp. 59–102. Kluwer.

Narens, L. (1980). On qualitative axiomatizations for probability theory. *Journal of Philosophical Logic 9*, 143–51.

Narens, L. (1981). On the scales of measurement. *Journal of Mathematical Psychology 24*(3), 249–75.

Narens, L. (1985). *Abstract Measurement Theory*. Massachusetts Institute of Technology Press.

Narens, L., and D. Luce (1993). Further comments on the 'nonrevolution' arising from axiomatic measurement theory. *Psychological Science 4*, 127–30.

Nolan, D. (1997). Impossible worlds: A modest approach. *Notre Dame Journal of Formal Logic 38*, 535–72.

Nolan, D. (2013). Impossible worlds. *Philosophy Compass 8*(4), 360–72.

Pfanzagl, J. (1968). *Theory of Measurement*. New York: Wiley.

Ramsey, F. (1931). Truth and probability. In R. Braithwaite (Ed.), *The Foundations of Mathematics and Other Logical Essays*, pp. 156–98. London: Routledge.

Reiss, J. (2016). *Error in Economics: Towards a More Evidence-Based Methodology*. Routledge.

Roberts, F. (1985). *Measurement Theory with Applications to Decisionmaking, Utility, and the Social Sciences*. Cambridge University Press.

Savage, L. J. (1954). *The Foundations of Statistics*. Dover.

Scott, D. (1964). Measurement structures and linear inequalities. *Journal of Mathematical Psychology 1*(2), 233–47.

Spohn, W. (1977). Where Luce and Krantz do really generalize Savage's decision model. *Erkenntnis 11*(1), 113–34.

Spohn, W. (1986). The representation of Popper measures. *Topoi 5*, 69–74.

Stalnaker, R. C. (1984). *Inquiry*. London: The Massachusetts Institute of Technology Press.

Stevens, S. (1946). On the theory of scales of measurement. *Science 103*(2684), 677–80.

Suppes, P. (1969). *Studies in the Methodology and Foundations of Science: Selected Papers from 1951 to 1969*. Dordrecht: Springer.

Suppes, P. (2014). Using Padoa's principle to prove the non-definability, in terms of each other, of the three fundamental qualitative concepts of comparative probability, independence and comparative uncertainty, with some new axioms of qualitative independence and uncertainty included. *Journal of Mathematical Psychology 60*, 47–57.

Suppes, P., and A. Pederson (2016). Qualitative axioms of uncertainty as a foundation for probability and decision-making. *Minds and Machines 26*, 185–202.

Suppes, P., and M. Zanotti (1976). Necessary and sufficient conditions for existence of a unique measure strictly agreeing with a qualitative probability ordering. *Journal of Philosophical Logic 5*(3), 431–8.

Suppes, P., and M. Zanotti (1982). Necessary and sufficient qualitative axioms for conditional probability. *Z. Wahrschelnllchkeltstheorle verw. Gebiete 60*, 163–9.

Suppes, P., and J. Zinnes (1963). Basic measurement theory. In D. R. Luce (Ed.), *Handbook of Mathematical Psychology*. John Wiley & Sons.

Swoyer, C. (1991). Structural representation and surrogative reasoning. *Synthese 87*(3), 449–508.

Titelbaum, M. (2022). *Fundamentals of Bayesian Epistemology 2: Arguments, Challenges, Alternatives*. Oxford University Press.

van Fraassen, B. (1976). Representation of conditional probabilities. *Journal of Philosophical Logic 5*, 417–30.

Wakker, P. (2004). On the composition of risk preference and belief. *Psychological Review 111*, 236–41.

Walley, P. (1991). *Statistical Reasoning with Imprecise Probabilities*. Chapman & Hall.

Zynda, L. (2000). Representation theorems and realism about degrees of belief. *Philosophy of Science 67*(1), 45–69.

Cambridge Elements ≡

Decision Theory and Philosophy

Martin Peterson
Texas A&M University

Martin Peterson is Professor of Philosophy and Sue and Harry E. Bovay Professor of the History and Ethics of Professional Engineering at Texas A&M University. He is the author of four books and one edited collection, as well as many articles on decision theory, ethics and philosophy of science.

About the Series

This Cambridge Elements series offers an extensive overview of decision theory in its many and varied forms. Distinguished authors provide an up-to-date summary of the results of current research in their fields and give their own take on what they believe are the most significant debates influencing research, drawing original conclusions.

Cambridge Elements ☰

Decision Theory and Philosophy

Printed in the United States
by Baker & Taylor Publisher Services